Attainment's

Aerobics *of the* Mind

MENTAL FITNESS PROGRAMMING FOR OLDER ADULTS

SUN MON TUES WED THURS FRI SAT

Be
Bet
Best
Board
Boosts
Bragged
Blunders

Roses are red,
Violets are blue,
Sugar is sweet
And so are you.

Revised edition

MARGE ENGELMAN

By Marge Engelman

Edited by Tom Kinney and Elizabeth Ragsdale

Graphic design by Elizabeth Ragsdale

ISBN: 1-57861-559-3
An Attainment Publication
©2006 Attainment Company, Inc. All Rights Reserved.
Printed in the United States of America.

Attainment Company, Inc.
P.O. Box 930160
Verona, Wisconsin 53593-0160
1-800-327-4269
www.AttainmentCompany.com

Contents

Contents

About the Author

Marge Engelman has been studying and teaching in the field of "learning in the older years" for 30 years. Her original research focused on encouraging the creative impulse in aging women.

She has a BA in Sociology, MA in Religious Education, MS in Environmental Design, and PhD in Adult Education. She has developed and taught "Aerobics of the Mind" and "Creativity in Aging" to groups in retirement centers, senior centers and adult daycare centers, and in workshops for leaders of these centers. She has lectured throughout Wisconsin and at national meetings on

topics related to learning in the later years. She has taught in the Graduate School of Education at the University of Wisconsin-Madison. She was a Governor's delegate from the state of Wisconsin to the White House Conference on Aging in 1995.

Marge is 77 years old and keeps her own mind active by auditing classes at the University of Wisconsin-Madison, designing innovative textile projects, growing gourds and developing them into works of art, and revising this book.

Comments, questions and reactions to the text are welcomed:

Marge Engelman
738 Seneca Place
Madison, WI 53711
e-mail: engelman@wisc.edu

Preface

Some years ago when I was doing research on creativity and aging with a group of women in their 70s, 80s and 90s, I asked them to take a test that would reveal the extent of their creative potential. Leone came to me and indicated that she couldn't do the test because she'd had a stroke. On the spur of the moment I suggested she try. And then I worried during the next hour and a half about whether or not it would be a discouraging experience for her, maybe even devastating. At the end of the allotted time Leone came out of the testing room with tears streaming down her face. I was disturbed, fearing the worst had happened. But then she smiled through the tears and said, "I'm crying because I just found out that my mind still works." I cried for joy with her.

That experience led me to thinking about all the older people who are convinced their mental ability has declined. I began to think about Aunt Margaret, age 80, who had just told me that she was too old to learn. I remembered Harry, who said, "You can't teach an old dog new tricks." I recalled all those birthday cards that poke fun and make puns about "over the hill after 40." I thought about my friends who were living life in a rut, doing the same old things in the same old way year after year. It seemed clear to me that many minds were going to waste.

So I decided to focus on what I had learned from Leone, who found out her mind still worked—even after a stroke. I read the works of Marion Diamond, a researcher at the University of California-Berkeley, who was challenging the many myths about the aging human brain. She asked, "Where did the statistic come from that we are losing 100,000 brain cells a day after 30?"

She noted that these claims had been made on the basis of autopsies of fewer than ten human brains and that the brains then available for autopsy tended to be those of unclaimed corpses, mostly the bodies of institutionalized men.

Diamond and other authors have recently concluded that the elderly brain is similar to the brain of a healthy young person. And that we can change the brain at any age, depending on how we use it. The evidence is accumulating that the brain works like a muscle; the harder you use it, the more it grows. Thus a good motto is: Use it or lose it.

Scientists are beginning to understand that even in old age the brain has a remarkable capacity to change and grow and that individuals have some control over how healthy and alert their brains remain as the years go by.

The exciting news today is that parts of the brain can regenerate themselves. What does that mean? With the aid of new technologies, such as positron emission tomography (PET) and magnetic resonance imaging (MRI) scanners, we can study how the brain functions. We know that the brain has as many as 100 billion neurons, many with 100,000 or more connections, called dendrites, through which they send signals to neighboring neurons. Even though we lose some neurons as we grow older, these neurons can sprout new dendrites late into life and thereby form new connections with one another.

Dr. Fred Gage of the Salk Instate in Lajolla, California, has shown in experiments with human brain tissue that "humans who were 65 or 70 years old were still producing new neurons and putting out branches that integrate into existing neural networks." This process, called neurogenesis, wasn't thought possible just five years ago.

The question of whether or not exercising your mind will help prevent Alzheimer's disease is getting a great deal of attention.

A study reported in a National Institute of Health press release on February 11, 2002, suggests that frequent participation in cognitively stimulating activities is associated with a reduced risk of Alzheimer's disease. Examples of stimulating activities considered in the study were reading, working crossword puzzles, playing card games and visiting museums. Results showed that an increase of one percentage point in these activities corresponded with a 33 percent reduction in the risk of Alzheimer's. The study followed over 700 dementia-free participants age 65 and older for an average of four and a half years.

An even more recent study, published in the prestigious *New England Journal of Medicine* (June 2003), was done in Einstein College of Medicine in New York City. In this study of 469 elderly people, those in the top third in mental activity had a 63 percent lower risk of dementia than those in the bottom third. Taking part in an activity one day a week reduced the risk by 7 percent.

Evidence is accumulating that challenging mental activity, such as aerobics-of-the-mind exercises, is crucial to keeping a healthy mind.

Many activities in senior education facilities promote personal growth, social well-being and physical wellness. But there are still many "leisure activities" offered to older adults in which they do not take part. They are more often passive spectators than active participants. There are lectures, slide programs and musical presentations during which they fall asleep. I have even heard some who are responsible for activities in a retirement center say they think their job is to "entertain" the older adults.

The purpose of this book is to foster a positive, upbeat attitude about the benefits of exercising the mind. Leaders and teachers of older adults, in groups and individually, will find abundant resources for encouraging the "well elderly" to keep their minds in shape. The ideas and activities discussed here will go beyond passive entertainment to encourage active participation. The reader will learn how to inspire others to stretch their thinking, try new and different ways of behaving, stimulate the memory and create a more creative brain.

Acknowledgments

It would have been impossible to write this book without the inspiration and feedback of hundreds of people who participated in classes, seminars, workshops and lectures where the ideas and activities included here were shared. Over 30 years ago a class I taught in creative textiles at a retirement center in Whitewater, Wisconsin, sparked the idea for this book. I was hooked when participants told me that they felt less depressed and had a reason to get up in the morning. The 40 women who were a part of my doctoral study on creative problem solving in aging women in Green Bay, Wisconsin were a very special group of people. These women exemplified how "nifty" growing older can be. Another group in the senior center at Belleville, Wisconsin willingly tried new ideas month after month, with good humor. Their coordinator, Betty Gill, was an enthusiastic co-conspirator.

Sally Benfarado has been a mentor, challenger and advisor over the many months of writing. Ruth Marion first suggested I write about what I was doing and offered helpful suggestions. A number of friends have been encouraging and supportive: Marilyn Slautterback, Jean Johnson, Elizabeth Nagle, Jane Danielson, Wes White, Greg Johll and Kari Berit Gustafson.

Acknowledgments

In the wings cheering me on have been my husband, Ken Engelman, and my daughter, Ann Engelman Yocom, who believed in me and this project.

In this revised edition of the book it was a pleasure to work with Elizabeth Ragsdale, who did the design and editing, and Tom Kinney, who did the final editing.

To all mentioned and many more unnamed, I am grateful.

Introduction

Aerobics of the mind is defined as stimulating and invigorating exercise for the brain. This book will show you how to put together unique programs that will challenge the well elderly to do mental aerobic exercises.

Part I, "Getting Started," describes a supportive environment for mental fitness activities and provides warm-up exercises.

Part II, "Model Programs," contains planned programs that can be used exactly as presented or varied as you choose.

I urge you to use the model programs in **Chapters 3, 4** and **5—"What Is Aerobics of the Mind?," "Our Marvelous Brains,"** and **"Have a Dream"**—since the information and exercises lay the groundwork for use of the material in Part III. The programs in **Chapters 6, 7** and **8—"Color, Wonderful Color," "Trees,"** and **"Will You Be My Valentine?"**—are presented as models of how to put together a 60- to 90-minute program of mental exercise.

Part III, "Exercises and Activities," is made up of chapters devoted to various kinds of mental aerobic exercises and activities from which you can pick and choose in developing your own routines. It is a compilation of ideas and materials I have developed and collected over a period of 30 years of working with older adults in community education programs, retirement centers, senior centers and adult daycare facilities.

Appendix A is devoted to **Pep Talks.** This section includes quotes, vignettes and other information you can use to reinforce the importance of keeping the mind active during aging. This material can be used before, during and after an aerobics-of-the-mind session. It provides rationale and support for the mental fitness workouts.

Appendix B includes the answers to all the games, quizzes and puzzles in the chapters.

Appendix C is an annotated listing of books, organizations and publications I have found useful as I have explored my way along the path to good mental stimulation.

How I decided what to include

Most of us who have done programming with older adults know that each group has its own personality, as does each individual. Thus your plans will be influenced by the abilities and interests of the group or individuals.

Each of us as leaders also has a unique personality and background of experiences that will influence our program planning. I have degrees in sociology, art, religious education and adult education, and you will see these influences creeping into the materials. I make no apologies for my biases. I confess that often when I am planning a session, I do things I feel like doing. Not only do I try to remember what the group likes and responds to, but I'm also aware that if I am enthused, my enthusiasm is contagious.

I have learned that sometimes when individuals tell me they really don't like a certain activity, a little nudging and cajoling can lead them to finding out how much they like it. For example, I enjoy looking at works of art by contemporary artists such as Picasso, Matisse and Rouault. Some of the art is quite abstract and illusive, and the first reaction by the group sometimes is, "We don't like that kind of thing." But with guidelines about what to look for in a painting, and with encouragement over a period of several months, this attitude can change. In one group when we focused on the print, American Gothic by Grant Wood, we spent a half-hour discussing the composition and intended meaning of the artist.

Here are key questions I ask myself about a given activity. Will it:

◈ Involve and challenge most members of the group?

◈ Stretch imaginations and encourage creativity?

◈ Promote doing new and different things?

◈ Foster busting routines and getting out of ruts?

◈ Stimulate thinking that looks forward rather than backward?

◈ Have carryover value in keeping minds active?

◈ Be fun?

Some readers may wish I had developed more programs in detail. Instead I have developed six model programs, three that lay the groundwork for doing aerobics of the mind and three that are typical of the kinds of programs you can develop. Part of the fun for you is to pick and choose exercises and activities from Part III and build your own programs based on your interests and those of your group members.

What is not included

Ideas for craft projects have not been included. Crafts can be mentally stimulating, but many other books and resources include these activities. A word of caution. Kits and "cut-and-dried" projects require little decision making on the part of the participants and are often of little mental aerobic value. It is important to differentiate between diversionary or "time filler" activities and those that encourage building a stronger and healthier mind.

This book contains few activities related to the performing arts, music or dance, all of which certainly can be mentally challenging. The emphasis here will be on explicit instruction related to thinking skills and mental fitness.

Just what is mentally stimulating?

Research on the brain is not advanced enough so that it can be said with absolute assurance that this or that activity will be the most mentally stimulating. Undoubtedly someday research will have found which parts of the brain are stimulated by which activities. Perhaps we will learn how to regenerate neurons and dendrites in specific parts of the brain where needed. But until then my tendency is to do a variety of activities that seem to have good potential for developing mental fitness.

My wish for you is that you will find good mental activity for your own brain as you work with these programs and exercises.

PART I

Getting Started

Creating the Climate

Creating a warm, inviting and supportive environment is crucial to successful aerobics-of-the-mind programs. This is done mainly through the physical setting and the facilitator.

The physical setting

The ideal arrangement is for the participants to sit around a table so that everyone can see the facilitator and each other. Each person should have a comfortable chair.

A chalkboard or flip chart and paper and pencils are basic equipment. Other needed items will become evident in the planned programs or specific exercises.

Adequate lighting and a quiet setting with a minimum of noise are important.

The facilitator

A good facilitator has these qualities:

◈ Is a warm and caring person who helps each person feel welcome and is genuinely interested in each participant.

◈ Learns everyone's name immediately and encourages others to learn the names of the group members.

◈ Is enthusiastic about the program and activities.

◈ Makes an effort to know what is important and unique to each individual.

◈ Thinks of learning as sharing and interacting rather than directing and controlling.

◈ Is willing to learn from participants.

◈ Respects all comments and contributions and finds a way to value them, helping each person feel treasured and building his or her self-esteem.

◈ Allows individuals to lead when there is the opportunity.

◈ Encourages persons to speak, but is diplomatic in setting limits if someone tends to dominate (see the following Ground Rules for Discussion).

◈ Has a sense of humor and encourages others in contributing humor.

◈ Knows how to nurture laughter.

◈ Finds ways to encourage persons to do new and different things even though they may be reticent.

◈ Asks for feedback at the end of a session, seeking out what participants liked and what they wished had been different.

Ground rules for discussion

Establishing and following a few basic ground rules will make the activities more pleasant for all:

◈ Each person's opinion counts.

◈ Everyone participates—no one dominates.

◈ One speaks; others listen.

◈ It's okay to disagree, but not to be disagreeable.

◈ Speak positively.

◈ Stay focused.

◈ Begin and end on time.[1]

Some special tips

One of the things I do to help learn names of group members is take each member's picture. I take several shots around the table so I can remember them as they were seated. Then I use small sticky notes to write the name of each person under his or her picture. I usually have extra photos made so I can give each person a copy. They love it.

Often one or more persons in a group has a hearing problem or has trouble seeing or difficulty writing. These disabilities should not dampen energy for doing aerobics-of-the-mind exercises. Members of the group can help each other, or perhaps an aide can be supportive to a person who needs help with hearing, seeing or writing.

I seldom use timed games. We have been brainwashed to believe that faster is better. Time pressure may have a small place in exercises such as those found in **Chapter 2, "Warm-Ups,"** but in general we need to give permission for participants to go at their own speed. Pressure usually creates stress, and stress is not the name of the game here.

Be sure to encourage group members to be leaders whenever possible. Give some thought to how the group could get along without you. The ultimate compliment to your leadership would be for them to decide they can survive quite well when you are not there.

Warm-Ups

I n this chapter you will find exercises that can be considered the mental equivalent of physical warm-ups. Think of these warm-ups as brushing the cob webs from the mind or clearing out the fog. Sometimes participants come to an activity period feeling sluggish or lethargic. An activity designed to wake up the mind and get the brain in gear is a valuable way to begin a session.

There are many ways to warm up such as doing physical exercises that include stretching and breathing, counting forward and backwards and reading upside down. These suggested activities are meant to encourage you to use your imagination and to develop routines that are appropriate to your group's abilities and interests.

A warm-up time should probably last no more than five to ten minutes.

Physical exercise

Stretching

Any number of stretching exercises are appropriate. There are many videotapes on the market that can guide your group through some basic stretching activities (see Appendix C). One of the groups I know best begins each session with a stretching time. They first used a video but then graduated to each person's choosing an exercise for the entire group to do together. An exercise is usually repeated eight to ten times.

Breathing

It is a good idea to include an exercise that focuses on breathing in the stretching session. It is surprising how few older adults really think about their breathing and its importance to their health. Ask the participants to sit up straight and take a deep breath. Then guide them in their breathing by saying: "Breathe in while I count to three; breathe out while I count to three." Continue to do this until they have established a comfortable rhythm. Andrew Weil, MD, and other experts on breathing indicate that the ideal pattern of breathing is to inhale as you count to four, hold your breath for a count of seven and then exhale as you count to eight. He indicates that it is not the speed with which you do the exercise, but the ratio of four, seven and eight for inhalation, hold and exhalation. Dr. Weil says that he teaches this exercise to almost all patients he sees and receives reports of remarkable benefits.[1]

Learning everyone's name

Your group members may know each other well, but if they do not, suggest that knowing each other's name is important. In addition to being a social nicety, it's good mental stimulation.

The participants sit in a circle or around a table. The first person gives his name. The second person repeats the name of the first person and then gives her own name. The third person repeats the names of the first and second persons and then gives his own name. This process is continued until all participants in the group have given their names and repeated the names, in order, of all those before them.

You may want to ask the first five persons to repeat all of the participants' names, since when they began there were not many names to remember.

A variation of this exercise is to ask each person to make a motion as he or she gives his or her name. Such motions might be blinking the eyes, pulling the ear, patting the top of the head, clapping the hands or snapping the fingers. These motions are then repeated as the names are repeated.[2]

Counting

Ask the participants to count out loud by twos up to 100 as fast as they can. (Usually speed is not encouraged, but in this warm-up exercise it may be acceptable.)

Then ask the participants to count backward from 100 to 1 as fast as they can. This exercise can be done as a group, although if the group is small and there is room, each person can go off by him or herself and do the counting, thus assuring that each person is getting the optimum challenge.

The alphabet

Ask each person to write down the letters of the alphabet, giving each letter a word partner such as *a*—ax, *b*—bell, *c*—cat, *d*—do and *e*—effort. Usually speed and timing are not necessary, but in this warm-up exercise it is good to ask the participants to do this as quickly as possible. The goal is to give the brain a brisk warm-up.

A variation of this exercise is to ask each person to choose one letter of the alphabet and list as quickly as possible any word that begins with the letter.

Animal names

Ask the participants to number from 1 to 20 and then to write beside each number the name of an animal such as 1—bear,

2—cow, 3—horse, 4—giraffe, continuing through 20. Doing this as quickly as possible is most stimulating to the brain.

This exercise can be varied using different categories, for example, vegetables, fruits, flowers, and names of men and women.

Let the words flow

Ask the participants to select a noun. It can be any noun that comes to mind. Tell them they have five minutes to write down as many phrases as possible that include or incorporate that noun. For example the noun "apple" might be chosen. Phrases that include apple might be apple crisp, apple pie, apple tree, apple core, Big Apple (New York), Adam's apple, taffy apple, Cranapple and so forth.

Tell the participants not to worry about spelling or whether or not their ideas are silly. The goal is to stimulate the brain to think as fast as it can. At the end of five minutes have them count their ideas. You might encourage them to notice if they have felt themselves getting warmer physically. Some people do feel their body temperature rising.

Upside-down reading

Give each of the participants some reading material and ask them to hold it upside down and try to read it. Since this is not our usual way to read, most people will have trouble doing this. However, it is good exercise for the brain as it struggles to make sense out of the words. Speed is not a concern in this exercise. Suggest that each person read as many sentences as possible until the brain feels challenged.

Imagining

This exercise is a mind stretcher that encourages the use of the imagination. Participants sit in a circle with paper and pencil. Ask the participants to stretch their imaginations and think of as many items as possible that can be:

◆ Put into a thimble.

◆ Filled with liquid.

◆ Hung on the living room wall.

◆ Used in cleaning a house.

◆ Sewed together.

You may want to use several of these imagination stretchers to begin a session. Be sure to develop some of your own ideas and ask the group members to develop some to be used another time.

Visualization

Visualization is the ability to create an idea or mental picture in your mind. For example, if the group is going to be working on an art project, the exercise might be for the group members to visualize themselves as working artists. You could lead them through a routine that might go something like this:

> Imagine yourself in a room you call your studio. You are surrounded by supplies such as paint brushes, tubes of paint, easels with canvas to paint on and a large color wheel on the wall with all the colors of the spectrum. There are many windows in the studio through which warm sunshine is streaming. There is soft music playing. You feel happy to be here and are confident of your abilities. You pick up a paint brush and begin to paint.

Adjust this exercise to fit your situation. There is evidence that visualizations such as this can actually have an impact on people's comfort level and ability to do things. To read more about this, consult *Creative Visualization* by Shakti Gawain (see **Appendix C**).

PART II

Model Programs

Model Programs

The goal of Part II is to give the program planner ideas about how sessions can be put together. Six sessions are included. As indicated in the **Introduction** to this book, I urge you to use the model programs in **Chapters 3, 4** and **5**—**"What Is Aerobics of the Mind?," "Our Marvelous Brains"** and **"Have a Dream"**—since the information and exercises lay the groundwork for use of the material in Part III. The programs in **Chapters 6, 7,** and **8**—**"Color, Wonderful Color," "Trees"** and **"Will You Be My Valentine?"**—are presented as models of how to put together a 60– to 90–minute program of mental exercise.

In preparation for doing a program, you should read the material through several times to become familiar with all the ideas and exercises. Then when you assist the group, put the concepts and directions into your own words.

There are often more ideas and exercises than you can use in a 60- to 90-minute session, so pick and choose based on your group's interests and abilities. You can also divide the material and use it in two or more sessions.

You might want to review **Chapter 1, "Creating the Climate,"** each time you do a program. I find that reminding myself over and over again about what it means to be a good facilitator helps to fix it in my mind and behavior.

Whenever I lead a group in doing aerobics-of-the-mind exercises, I am aware that I am also stimulating and stretching my own mind. Often the kinds of things we do result in unexpected joys. For instance, when I encouraged a senior center group to write original Valentine verses, Anna, who usually had nothing to contribute, came up with this rhyme: "Roses are red, violets are blue. Your feet stink and so do you." We giggled and laughed and praised her creation. Anna's usually dull eyes began to sparkle. I think we made her day; she certainly added joy to ours.

What Is Aerobics of the Mind?

This first model program is designed to help you and your group understand some of the basic ideas of aerobics of the mind. Instead of simply listing and explaining exercises, I have included some narrative background information that helps explain why we do these kinds of activities. Spend some time becoming familiar with this material so that you can put it into your own words.

There are enough exercises in this program to fill two or more sessions, perhaps three, depending on the time you have. This abundance of materials will allow you to pick and choose what fits your group best. It is presented as one program because it forms good background for further sessions on aerobics of the mind. I have used the material included here a number of times in workshops and in speeches, and find that people appreciate it and enjoy themselves.

Aerobic exercise

We are learning that how we use our minds has a lot to do with how we age.

Evidence is accumulating that the brain works much like a muscle. The harder you use it, the more it grows and the healthier it is.

In recent years most of us have become convinced that we need to keep our bodies active by walking, swimming, biking, jogging and dancing. We've learned that aerobic exercise, getting the heartbeat up to a certain speed, is important.

Begin by asking the participants: "How many of you make a point of getting some form of aerobic exercise? every day? twice a week? once a week?" (This is not meant to engender guilt feelings but to raise awareness of aerobic exercise.)

Now let's talk about aerobics of the mind—giving the brain a workout. Ask participants about the last time they made an effort to stretch their thinking, try something totally new, do something creative. When was the last time they took on a new learning project? When did they last work up a sweat thinking?

Discussion Our brains can change

Scientists used to believe the brain was hard-wired by adolescence and inflexible in adulthood. But researchers are discovering that the brain has the ability to change and adapt throughout life. Best of all, this research has opened up an exciting world of possibilities for treating patients with strokes and head injuries, and perhaps warding off Alzheimer's disease.

So, we can no longer say, "You can't teach an old dog new tricks" or "It's all downhill after 30." Most of us should expect to keep our youthful mental powers as we enter our 60s, 70s, 80s and beyond.

Exercise Exercising our minds with illusions

What do you see in this image? What else
do you see? Can you see both at once?

What do you see in this image? Can you see
the old woman? Can you see the young woman?

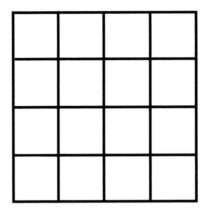

How many squares do you see? Continue to look and see if you can find more squares.

These exercises (taken from **Chapter 14, "Fun with Optical Illusions"**) show how we tend to see what is obvious and fail to look beyond or press ourselves to see differently. We tend to get in ruts about how we see things.

Exercise Folding our hands and arms

How we fold our hands and arms gives us clues about getting in ruts. Ask the participants to follow these directions:

> Fold your hands with the fingers positioned between each other. Now look to see which thumb is over the top. Raise your hand if the left thumb is over the top. Raise your hand if the right thumb is over the top.

(Usually there will be about an equal number of participants who have used each position.)

> Now try folding your hands the opposite way.

(This usually brings expressions of surprise because many find it difficult to do it the opposite way.)

Fold your arms. Observe which arm is over the top, right or left?

(Again the group is usually about equally divided for each position. Some will observe that the left thumb was over the top, but that the right arm was over the top.)

Now try folding your arms the opposite way.

(Again there will be expressions of surprise.)

What does all this mean? We are not totally sure. It may have something to do with right brain/left brain tendencies. There is some suspicion that those who put the left thumb over the top may have originally been left handed. We do not know for sure what these inclinations mean, but one thing this exercise shows us is that we get in ruts about how we do things.

Discussion What are the ruts in our lives?

Let's reflect on some of the things we tend to do the same way every time we do them. What about our getting-up-in-the-morning routines? Do we always follow the same patterns? What about our going-to-bed routines? Do we always set the table exactly the same way? When we go to the store do we always take the same route?

The point of this discussion is that "routine busting" can be stimulating to the brain. Doing things differently can spark the mind.

Exercise The Small Cage Habit

There is a story about a very sad bear kept in a very small cage in the town zoo.

Have a member of the group read the short story "The Small Cage Habit" (page 38). Another possibility is for each member to have in hand a card with the story printed on it. The card can then be taken home and serve as a reminder to try new and different things.

The Small Cage Habit

Once upon a time there was a very sad polar bear who was kept in a very small cage in the town zoo. When the sad bear wasn't eating or sleeping, she occupied her time pacing . . . eight paces forward and eight paces back again. Again and again she paced the parameters of her very small cage.

One day the zookeeper said: "It's depressing to see this bear pacing back and forth in her confining cage. I shall build her a great open and elegant space so that she may romp with great freedom and abandon." And so he did.

As the space was completed, great waves of excitement charged through the town, and finally the magic day came to move the bear to her new headquarters. The town mayor delivered a rousing speech, with a chorus of children screaming in anticipation.

The city marching band manifested a brassy bravado of sound that reached a crescendo at the glorious moment that the sad bear was ushered into her elegant new quarters. Whispers of curious expectation rose from the crowd as they watched the great beast frozen in the uncertainty of the moment. The sad bear looked to her left and to her right, and then she began to move . . . one step, two, five, eight paces forward and eight back again . . . again and again. To the shocked amazement of the crowd, she still paced the parameters of her old very small cage.[1]

As a way to imprint in our minds the message of the story "The Small Cage Habit," let's stand up, find a place in the room to call our own and step off the eight steps forward and eight steps back again.

You, the leader, can count:

One, two, three, four, five, six, seven, eight and then one, two, three, four, five, six, seven, eight steps back again.

A kind of rhythm can be developed that will reinforce the story in the minds of the participants.

Exercise Connecting the dots

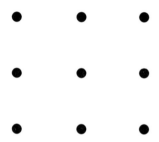

Without lifting your pencil from the paper, draw four straight, connected lines that go through all nine dots, but through each dot only once.
After you have tried two different ways, ask yourself what restrictions you have set up for yourself in solving this problem.

Give the group members six to eight minutes to work on this puzzle taken from **Chapter 18, "Puzzles and Numbers."** Most people have trouble doing it unless they have done it before. The problem is that we tend to see the nine dots as a box and feel we must "stay inside the lines." The key is to go outside the lines twice (see **Appendix B** for the answer).

Discussion Connecting the dot exercise

Why do you think we had so much trouble doing this exercise? Did we box ourselves in? When told to ask ourselves what restrictions we have set up, most of us still limit ourselves.

Conclusion

We have explored some basic ideas related to aerobics of the mind. We have tried to explain what it is. We have done some exercises that stretched our minds. (Depending on your style and the value you find in reviewing the exercises, you may or may not want to briefly review the session.)

Our Marvelous Brains

Introduce this session by holding in your hand a cantaloupe or honeydew melon that weighs approximately three pounds. As you hold it for all to see, share some or all of the following information, putting it into your own words, if possible:

◈ The brain is made up of about three pounds of gray/pink jelly.

◈ The brain is probably the most complicated piece of equipment in the universe.

◈ Ironed out, it would be roughly the size of a sheet of newsprint.

◈ To fit into the skull it has to be highly convoluted.

◈ The critical mass of the human brain is the cerebral cortex, the outer layer of the brain.

◈ The cerebral cortex contains three-fourths of the neurons in the brain and is the seat of thinking, judgment, speech and memory (it's what makes us human).

◈ The complexity of the human brain lies in the vast number of synapses (connections) between brain cells.

◈ The number of interconnections among the cells is beyond the human imagination.

◈ Researchers estimate that the normal brain has a quadrillion connections between the brain cells, more than all the phone calls made in the United States in the past decade.[1]

As you share this information, you may want to pass the melon to group members so that each has a chance to sense the weight of the brain and to marvel at all that goes on in this fairly small organ of the body.

Neurons, dendrites, axons and synapses

Sketch an enlarged diagram of neurons, dendrites and axons on the chalkboard or flip chart, labeling the different parts. Don't worry if your sketch is not perfect because all that's needed is to give a basic idea of the cells in the brain.

Ask the participants to look at the sketch and to picture as best they can some ten billion neurons each receiving connections from perhaps a hundred others, each of which is connected with a hundred others. Tell the group that there are more neurons in the brain than there are stars in the Milky Way and that the brain has the information processing power of a *hundred billion* medium-sized interacting computers.

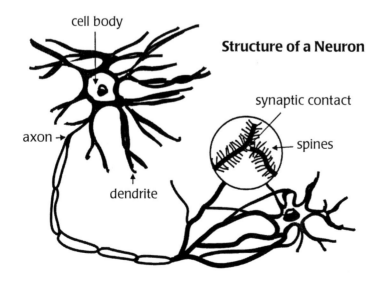

cell body

Structure of a Neuron

synaptic contact

axon →

spines

dendrite

You may want to repeat some of this information several times. Admit that it is difficult to comprehend. The goal is to inspire in the group a sense of wonder and awe about the brain.

Exercise Draw neurons and dendrites

As a way to help participants fix in their memories this information about neurons and dendrites, give them paper, pencils, crayons and colored pencils or pens and ask that they draw several neurons with dendrites. Suggest that it would make an interesting pattern if they were to draw and color as many neurons and dendrites as possible on one sheet of paper. Assure them that there is no expectation that the drawings be especially artistic or even accurate, but that the point is to help the memory hold onto these images.

Test your brain power

You can use this true/false quiz to further enhance the participants' knowledge about the brain. The quiz could be photocopied so that each person has a copy, or the statements could be read by you or a volunteer from the group. The participants could simply number from one to eight and write true or false for each statement. (This quiz was adapted from information in *Boost Your Brain Power* by Ellen Michaud, Russell Wild and the Editors of *Prevention*.)[2]

1. After about age 40–50, you can expect your mental powers to decline.
2. Memory loss is a natural part of the aging process.
3. Chronic confusion and forgetfulness are the first symptoms of approaching senility.
4. There is nothing you can do to slow the aging of your brain.
5. Once dendrites are lost, they cannot be regenerated.
6. Creative ability cannot be developed in aging persons.
7. Once your memory "goes," nothing can bring it back.
8. Males are more creative than females.

When the participants have completed the quiz, review the brief answers and explanations in **Appendix B.**

Left brain/right brain

Briefly share this information with the participants:

> In the early 1960s Dr. Roger Sperry and his colleagues did research on a 48-year-old person with epilepsy. Because the patient suffered severe seizures, the physicians severed the corpus callosum—the connection between the left brain and the right brain. What they learned is that the brain has two sides and that the sides tend to function differently.
>
> The left hemisphere tends to work with facts and is logical and rational. It works with diagrams and data and sees letters. Language is learned here. The right hemisphere deals with feelings, imagination, intuition, creativity. The right side sees mental images and colors, and is tuned into rhythm. It tends to be the artistic side.

Assure the group that it is not quite as simple as this, and new research is showing that both sides may be involved in different ways in different people. However, we can capitalize on the fact that learning in general is easier, faster and more fun when we involve both sides of the brain.

Exercise *Rhythm and music*

A good way to show that we learn and remember best when both sides of the brain are involved is to ask the participants to sing the song we all learned to memorize the alphabet. Begin by singing and have them join in:

> ABCDEFG, HIJKLMNOP, QRSTU and V, WX and Y and Z.
> Now I know my ABCs; next time won't you sing with me?

Some members may have learned a slightly different wording or ending.

Ask the group members why they think we all remember this ABC song. They will have their own ideas, but an important contributor to our memory is that the letters are a left brain activity, while the rhythm and music is a right brain activity. When both sides of the brain are used, memory is reinforced.

As another illustration, ask the group members to repeat the verse most of us use to help us remember the names of the months and how many days are in each month:

> Thirty days have September, April, June and November. All the rest have 31, excepting February, which has but 28 in time, 'til leap year gives it 29.

Point out that the rhythm and the words and numbers used together help us remember.

Ask the participants if they can think of other examples where words and music or rhythm reinforce each other.

Exercise *Using our double mind*

Ask the participants to take a piece of paper and pencil and number from 1 to 12. Then ask them to list 12 words that describe how they think about themselves.

Next ask the participants to put aside the first list and take another sheet of paper, but this time put the pencil in their nondominant hand, the hand with which they normally do not write, and number from 1 to 12. Ask again that they write 12 words that they feel describe themselves. This will be awkward and slow going for most. Suggest that there is no need to try to remember what they wrote on the first list. The lists may be quite different.

When all have finished, ask them to compare their two lists. In what ways are they alike? In what ways are they different? Usually people report a variety of differences such as: Words in the first list tend to be longer, more abstract; words in the second list tend to be shorter, more earthy, more emotional.

Tell them that information for each list came from different sources in their brain. The first list came from the left hemisphere or the dominant hemisphere for language and conceptual thought. The second list originated in the right hemisphere, which specializes in imagery and emotional expressions.[3]

How to make your dendrites grow

Introduce this exercise by telling the participants that researchers are indicating that if we want to make our dendrites grow, it is important to do new and different things. Let's imagine that we are setting a goal of doing at least one thing differently every day. Here are some examples of simple ordinary daily activities that would lend themselves to change:

◈ Set the table in a different way.

◈ Fix your hair in a new way.

◈ Wear some jewelry you forgot you had.

◈ Try a new recipe.

◈ If you walk, take a different route.

◈ Phone someone you've never phoned before.

◈ Plan a surprise for someone.

◈ Visit a place you have never been before.

Now ask the participants what ideas they have of things they might do differently. Ask them to write down some ideas that come to mind. The participants may want to be more specific about the ideas you suggested, but hopefully they will be original and surprise themselves with their creative ideas. After they have had some time to think and write, ask them to share their thoughts.

Ask if they would be willing to try out several of their ideas before your next session and let the group know what they did and how they felt about what they did. This is an exercise that can be done over and over again to good advantage. Assure them that these activities will make their dendrites grow and will perk up their lives.

Exercise Brainstorming

If there is time, conclude the session with a brainstorming activity. Point out that one of the best ways to use our brains and foster creativity is to do brainstorming (see **Chapter 10, "Creative Problem Solving,"** for the rules of brainstorming).

Ask the participants to number from 1 to 25 on a sheet of paper and think up new uses for a paper clip. Encourage them to go beyond 25 new uses if possible. After all have exhausted their ideas, ask the group members to share by writing the new uses on the chalkboard.

Conclusion

I realize that there are more exercises and ideas here than you would need for a 60- or 90-minute session. Pick and choose what you will use or perhaps use the materials for two sessions.

Have a Dream

Begin the session by using some of the following ideas. Put them into your own words and add some words of your own.

This program was inspired by Arthur Fleming, former Social Security Administration Commissioner who served in the administration of five United States Presidents. At age 90, he spoke at the White House Conference on Aging in May 1995. One of his most memorable lines was: "We must value our memories, *but we must also have a dream.*" He went on to say:

> I have a dream that this national community will only go forward, not backward, in helping our people deal with the hazards and vicissitudes of life. . . . I don't know what amount of time is left to me, but I am going to do my best to draw on my memory to fuel the action that is needed in order to realize that dream.

Here is a man at 90 saying we must have a dream. His dream is broad and far ranging, but a dream can also be a specific, short-range dream or goal. His comments set me to thinking about whether or not I have dreams for my future.

We have been conditioned to believe that young people should have dreams, but we seldom speak of older persons having a dream. For many of us our dream has been to "take it easy" in our later years. We say to ourselves that there isn't anything we *have* to do. That may be true, but does that attitude make for a healthy, happy way to grow older? Maybe for some it does. But others of us believe that we can dream new dreams and set new goals.

The research is showing that doing new and different things is more stimulating to the brain than the repetition of what we've always done. In the last several years I have been learning how to make paper and find it a fun and challenging activity. I am also trying to learn how to cross-country ski but having difficulty coordinating my feet and brain.

Let's assume that the participants in your group have some interest in having a dream, or at least setting some goals for the future. How do we go about helping them? Here are a few ideas; you will think of other ways.

Keep in mind that these can be straightforward good aerobics-of-the-mind exercises. On the other hand these exercises can be a positive, life-enhancing experience. To have a dream is to have hope. To have a dream is to have a reason for getting up in the morning. To have a dream can give new meaning to life.

Discussion Dream a dream

Remind the participants that in our newspapers and magazines and on television almost every week we learn about people who in late life are doing interesting things they have never done before. Ask the group members to think of these stories. Or perhaps they know people who are daring to try new activities in their older years. Perhaps they have been experimenting with some new activities. Ask them to share these stories.

Have some ideas in your own mind such as the 73-year-old woman who, after the death of her husband, decided to take ballroom dancing lessons and went on to win recognition nationwide for her skills. Or the older woman who bought a new set of dinnerware (she lived to the age of 103). Or how about the older couple who after retirement bought a Harley Davidson motorcycle and traveled throughout the country. These are fairly unusual activities for older people, but there are many more ordinary dreams that older people have dreamed, such as:

◆ Being in touch with a long lost family member.

◆ Growing a plant one has never grown before.

◆ Planning a different kind of party.

◆ Becoming a grandparent to a child who has none.

◆ Joining a literacy group and teaching a child to read.

◆ Learning a new language.

◆ Taking piano lessons.

◆ Writing memories of one's life for one's family.

◆ Enriching one's spiritual life.

◆ Joining a Gray Panther group.

◆ Getting a pet.

Exercise Dreams from our youth

Ask the participants if, when they were young, they had dreams about what they might like to be or do. These could be big dreams or smaller dreams. Ask them to share their thoughts and have a group member write the dreams on the chalkboard.

Now ask the group members, "What prevented you from following through on your early aspirations?" There will be many good reasons such as finances, disapproval by parents, marriage, children, illness, a war, or life taking a different turn than expected.

Suggest participants keep these dreams of their youth in mind as they continue to think about possible dreams and goals for their lives today. Suggest that these early yearnings may still have some potential for the years ahead.

Exercise A new dream or goal

Ask the participants to list their dreams on a piece of paper numbered from 1 to 10. These can be big dreams or smaller dreams or goals. Review the rules for brainstorming found in **Chapter 10, "Creative Problem Solving."** After each person has listed as many possible dreams as he or she can, ask each to share some ideas with the group.

This activity may not come easily for some participants since it may be a totally new concept to envision dreams and goals. Be patient and encouraging.

Exercise Steps to accomplish the dream or goal

Ask each participant to pick one idea and write it at the top of the back side of the paper and again number from 1 to 10. Ask them to decide what concrete steps they might take to carry out this dream or goal. If you choose, the participants could take home their list, making a commitment to report back on their progress.

The above exercises may be all that you want to use, but here are several more ideas that may encourage participants to have a dream.

Exercise What is it that you would really like to do?

In this exercise the facilitator begins by asking a volunteer to discuss what it is that she would really like to do. The facilitator asks the volunteer the same question, "What is it that you would really like to do?" The question should be asked at least three times, maybe more, depending on the comfort level of the volunteer. Each time the volunteer will answer the question in the best way she can. The idea is that continually asking the same question over and over will evoke some interesting insights from the responder.

After this demonstration, ask the group members to divide themselves in pairs and take turns asking each other the question, "What is it that you really want to do?" After all have had time to work on this, ask the participants to share ideas that may be useful to them.

If the group is willing, ask that the members continue to dialogue in pairs, this time asking the question, "What is it that keeps you from doing what you really want to do?"

Exercise If you could live your life over

As a concluding exercise, ask the participants to write down these words: "If I could live my life over I would. . . ." Then ask that they complete the sentence. Suggest that they may want to try out several ways to complete the sentence. Indicate that they are to think in terms of no barriers, no lack of money, no time limits, no concern for what others think.

A warning about this activity: It may be disturbing to some, so be sensitive to that potential and provide an "out" for those who would rather not do it.

Color, Wonderful Color

Throughout history color has been important to humans. It has been studied from many perspectives: Historical, biological, psychological and visual. Our lives are greatly enriched by color. Can you imagine living in a world where there was no color? What would it be like living in a world where everything was white? Or what about a world where all objects were black? This program will help us appreciate what an important element color is in our lives.

Discussion Thoughts and feelings about color

Begin the discussion by asking questions such as:

◈ What is your favorite color and why?

◈ When you buy a new blouse or shirt, what color are you likely to choose?

◈ Has your choice of colors for clothing changed over the years?

◈ How does purple make you feel?

◈ How about yellow, green, pink?

Bring a collection of fabrics such as red velveteen, pink chiffon, white net, green brocade, black felt, gold satin, red-checked gingham and blue denim. As you hold up a piece of fabric, ask the participants what it makes them think of.

Exercise Hearing a poem—writing a poem

Read the poem "What Is Purple?" to the participants.

Give the participants paper and pencil and ask them to agree on a color and write about it, following the format of "What Is Purple?" Suggest that they use short sentences. When they have had some time to work on their own, encourage each person to contribute one or two favorite lines to write on a large sheet of paper. This can be called a "group poem."

Pick a second color and follow the same format. Try a third color if the group members are having fun.

Exercise A color collage

Ask the participants to put together a collage using pictures cut from magazines. A first effort might be to do a collage having one or two colors as a focus, such as varying shades of blue or green. A second suggestion would be to choose pictures that basically use the primary colors—red, yellow and blue. A 12-inch square of cardboard would be a good background on which to paste the collage.

If the group members are willing, exhibit the collages where all can see and enjoy them.

Exercise Weaving with color

A fun way to focus on color and increase appreciation of color is to do some weaving with paper. Hand and brain coordination will be exercised.

Have available a package of 9-by-12-inch construction paper in a variety of colors, scissors, rulers, pencils and rubber cement or other

What Is Purple?

by Mary O'Neill

Time is purple
Just before night
When most people
Turn on the light—
But if you don't it's
A beautiful sight.
Asters are purple,
There's purple ink.
Purple's more popular than you think. . . .
It's sort of a great
Grandmother to pink.
There are purple shadows
And purple veils,
Some ladies purple
Their fingernails.
There's purple jam
And purple jell
And a purple bruise
Next day will tell
Where you landed
When you fell.
The purple feeling
Is rather put-out
The purple look is a
Definite pout.
But the purple sound
Is the loveliest thing
It's a violet opening
In the spring.[1]

paste. (I personally like rubber cement since it is forgiving—pieces of paper can be moved.)

Ask the participants to cut three different colored sheets of paper into one-inch strips. Using a ruler and a pencil, mark off the nine inches on the short end of the paper and then cut the length of the paper on those one-inch marks. Each participant will then have 27 one-inch wide strips of paper—nine strips of each color.

Ask that they lay out seven one-inch strips on the table with about one-quarter inch between the pieces. The next step is to begin to weave the remaining strips, over and under the strips laid out on the table. They may choose any color combinations they like. Weaving the first several strips is the most difficult, but it gets easier after that. When they have woven at least eight or nine strips into the original seven, suggest that they add to the original strips.

As the participants go along, they will have ideas of how to do the weaving differently. Encourage them to take apart the original weaving and to try new color combinations. As they do this, suggest that they observe how some colors may seem to change, perhaps be more intense or more dull, depending on what colors are next to them. Ask the group members to observe what color combinations they like best, noting that most everyone has favorite colors.

As the exercise begins to wind down, suggest that they may want to glue some of the pieces in the weaving so that they can be permanently fastened and will not come apart. If the group members are so inclined, you could display these "wonderful weavings" on a bulletin board or wall, labeling the display "Studies in Color." Some may observe that they did exercises like this when they were children. Affirm that to be true, and add that our brains still need that kind of stimulation to stay healthy.

Discussion New insights about color

Conclude with a discussion of what participants have learned about color in this session.

Trees

I love trees. I love their presence, their stature, the way they stand and hold dominion. I love the character that a tree conveys. I love to see them anew each new season. I love to look at them, to be among them, to sit under them, to look up at them.

This quote from Jane Danielson, a former student at the University of Wisconsin, is a good way to begin a session that focuses on trees. Jane developed a two-day class on appreciating trees, and some of her ideas are included here.

Often we take trees for granted. This session will help you and the group look at trees in new ways, observe more carefully, and stir new thoughts and feelings about these marvelous gifts of nature. It is best if these exercises are done outside among the trees, but they can be done indoors with the exception of Get to Know a Tree.

There is more material than you will need for one session, so choose activities that seem best suited to your group, or do several sessions on trees.

Exercise Listing the names of trees

Begin with sharing some basic information about trees such as:

> The tree is the largest of all plants. But trees can also be
> very small, like dwarf trees that grow naturally in arctic
> regions. There are about 2,000 kinds of trees. More than
> 1,000 grow in the United States. Most trees belong to one
> of two main groups—the broadleaf trees and the needle
> leaf trees. The oldest trees are California's giant sequoias.
> The oldest sequoias are about 3,500 years old.[1]

Now begin the exercise by asking, "How many trees do you think we
can name?" Ask the group members to make a guess as to how many
trees they can list.

Then using a chalkboard or flip chart, write down this number
and begin to list the names of the trees with everyone participating.
Usually the group members will underestimate how many they can
name and will be surprised at the members' recall of the names
of trees.

Exercise Timeline indicating significant trees

Ask the participants to think of trees they associate with different
events or phases of their life—childhood, teenage years, early
adulthood, later adulthood, present day. Suggest that they think in
terms of where they played, vacations, special events and places
where they lived. The timeline can be developed on an $8^1/_2$-by-11-
inch piece of paper, by drawing a line lengthwise and writing the
years above that line. The names of the trees they recall can then
be written below the line.

It may take a little time to get into this exercise, but when the idea
begins to "click," it will be a stimulating and invigorating activity.

Exercise A tree is like a poem

Ask the participants if they remember the poem "Trees" by Joyce Kilmer. Many people memorized this when they were young. In case some do not remember the poem, have copies available. (It can be found in *Best Loved Poems of the American People* by Hazel Felleman.) Ask the group members to repeat the poem together several times, permitting the words to speak to them.

Ask the participants if they have any special memories about learning this poem, such as when they planted a tree on Arbor Day. Discuss what the poem means to them.

Now ask the participants to try their hand at writing a four-line poem of their own about trees. Suggest that the first two lines rhyme and that the last two lines rhyme.

Exercise If you could be a tree

Ask the participants to give some thought to the question: "If you could be a tree, what tree would you choose to be?" What characteristics does your tree have that appeals to you?

Exercise Get to know a tree

This activity needs to be done outside in a park or any place where there are trees. Participants will need paper and pencil and a firm surface on which to write.

Tell the participants that this is an opportunity to get to know a tree in a meaningful way. Suggest that they begin by looking at the tree from afar so they can see as much of it as possible. Ask that they write everything they can about the tree—its color, shape, bark, leaves and shadow, if there is one. Ask them to jot down their observations and thoughts.

Continue with these suggestions:

1. Move as close to the tree as you can.
2. Stand or sit under it.
3. Look up into the tree as though you were the trunk.
4. Note your observations and impressions of the tree from this perspective.
5. Then smell the tree, feel it, pick a leaf and observe it carefully, and put your arms around the tree with your ear up against the trunk and try to hear the sap running. (It may be difficult to hear the sap running unless the environment is very quiet.)

Again, have the participants write down their observations and thoughts.

When the participants return from this time with their chosen tree, ask for volunteers to read parts of what they have written. Ask the group members to reflect on the experience. How did they feel? What did they learn? Has it made any difference in how they now see trees?

Exercise Artists' portrayals of trees

Ask the participants to search in magazines and books for pictures of trees. Photographs are fine, but drawings by artists can bring some new insights. The photos and drawings can provide the background for a good discussion about how trees have been portrayed by artists and photographers. Artists often have the ability to sense the most unique characteristics of a tree and to portray it in a sketch, painting or photograph. An exercise like this can sharpen observations, perspectives and appreciation of trees.

Exercise A rubbing of tree bark

The goal of this activity is to explore the nature of tree bark and to enhance appreciation of the textures of bark on a variety of trees.

Provide thin but sturdy paper and charcoal or crayons so that participants can do a rubbing of the bark of a tree. Ideally this could be done outside with the members choosing their own tree, or perhaps several trees. However, if it is not possible to go outdoors, ask the participants to bring pieces of bark to class. Rubbings are most revealing if the piece of bark is at least four inches by four inches, but smaller pieces will work also.

Conclusion

To conclude this session, encourage the participants to discuss new insights about trees that they have gained during this time focusing on nature's largest plants.

Will You Be My Valentine?

As background for this session ask the participants to recall history or information about why we celebrate Valentine's Day. Encourage them to remember information such as:

There are many different stories about the beginnings of Valentine's Day. Some say that it began with an ancient Roman festival. Others connect the day with one or more saints of the early Christian Church. Still other sources think that it was related to an old English belief that birds mated on this day.

A favorite story says that Valentine was an early Christian who made friends with many children. He was imprisoned by the Romans because he refused to worship their god. The children missed him so much that they wrote loving notes and put them between the bars of his cell window. This story may explain why we send messages of love on Valentine's Day. A number of stories say that Valentine was killed on February 14, and some years after that, about 500 AD, the Pope named February 14 as St. Valentine's Day.[1]

Discussion Valentine's Day, then and now

Take some time for participants to share their memories of
Valentine's Day when they were young. However, do not dwell
totally on the past. Suggest that they share what they do now on
Valentine's Day.

Exercise Heart-shaped puzzle

As the participants arrive, give them heart-shaped puzzles to fit
together. Prepare the puzzles ahead of time using red or white
construction paper glued to lightweight cardboard. Draw heart
shapes that are approximately four by five inches and then cut
them into five or six pieces. Instead of doing this yourself, you may
want to ask several members of the group to make the puzzles. As
the puzzles are made, try putting them back together so that you or
your helpers experience the degree of difficulty. How challenging
you want to make them will depend on your group members.
Usually participants like working together in twos or threes on
puzzles, but they could work individually as well.

Exercise A Valentine poem

Begin by asking the group members to recite the traditional
Valentine poem:

> Roses are red,
> Violets are blue,
> Sugar is sweet
> And so are you.

Provide paper and pencil and ask that they write the first two
lines: "Roses are red, Violets are blue." Then ask that they write
two original lines to finish the verse. Suggest that they stretch their
brains to write four of five such verses. When they have run out of

ideas, ask that they share several of their creations. This exercise is not too difficult and lots of fun.

If the group members are on a roll and enjoying writing poetry, suggest that they write one or more original four-line poems appropriate for Valentine's Day.

Exercise A red memory

Since red is the color most associated with Valentine's Day, challenge the group members to think red by using this exercise.

Write on the chalkboard these headings:

◆ Vegetables   ◆ Places

◆ Fruits   ◆ People

◆ Flowers   ◆ Expressions

◆ Birds

If space is limited, you may want to write only one heading at a time. Then ask the participants to begin by naming all the vegetables that are red or have red on them. Continue to do this with fruits, flowers and birds. Then move to places, people and expressions that contain the word red in their title, name or words. This is a winner for maximum brain stimulation.

Exercise Appreciating a painting

Review **Chapter 13, "Art Appreciation."** Choose a work of art that may have some relationship to a love theme such as Picasso's *Mother and Child,* one of Chagall's paintings with a woman or a couple floating in the sky, Edward Hicks's *Peaceable Kingdom* or any work that seems appropriate to you. Decide on the approach you will use to help participants understand and appreciate the work of art. If in doubt, use the tried and true approach by listing on the chalkboard What To Look for in Works of Art found in Chapter 13.

Exercise An act of kindness

Lead the participants in thinking of acts of kindness they can do on Valentine's Day. Use the brainstorming technique found in **Chapter 10, "Creative Problem Solving."** Review the simple rules for brainstorming. There are many little books that can be an inspiration for this exercise, for example, *Random Acts of Kindness* and *More Random Acts of Kindness* by the editors of Conari Press in Berkeley, California. I have on occasion read several vignettes from these books or asked participants to read them as a way to prime the pump so ideas will flow.

When the group members have listed a number of possible acts of kindness on the chalkboard, ask if they are willing to make a commitment to carrying out several of these acts. You will be amazed at the fluency of ideas that will come and the enthusiasm that can be generated. This is an exercise that might be used at other times of the year as well. Giving to others invigorates the brain and gives new life.

Exercise A picture takes the place of a word

Ask the participants to write a love letter replacing words with pictures (see **Chapter 12, "Right Brain Exercises,"** for directions). When each person has exerted some effort on this exercise, ask the group members to pass their love letters to the person on their right to see if it can be read and understood.

Conclusion

As a way to end this session, ask the participants what love songs they remember and then sing several of them together. Never mind if you don't have a piano for accompaniment or if many people sing off key. The stimulation is in remembering the words and the tunes.

Some love songs that older people tend to remember are "Let Me Call You Sweetheart," "I Love You Truly" and "Because." Some that may not be quite as familiar are "With Someone Like You," "It's a

Hundred to One I'm in Love," "Miss You" and "People Will Say We're in Love."

As you may have noted, this is a program with a traditional theme, Valentine's Day, that uses some of the activities found in Part III. The program is an example of how to pluck ideas from the chapters in Part III and with some modifications mold them into traditional theme programs. This can be done for many other theme programs, for example, Thanksgiving, Christmas, Halloween, St. Patrick's Day, New Year's Day, Fourth of July or President's Day. You will find that organizing programs in this way helps keep your own mind active!

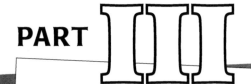

PART III

Exercises
and
Activities

Exercises and Activities

This section of the book is made up of chapters devoted to many kinds of mental aerobic exercises from which you can pick and choose in developing your own programs. Here you will find a compilation of ideas and materials that have been developed and collected over a period of 30 some years of working with older adults in community education programs, retirement centers, senior centers and adult daycare facilities.

Every setting of older adults is different and has its own unique characteristics. Usually group members have favorite activities and special ways of doing things. Some of the exercises suggested may seem odd or quite foreign, and some individuals may offer resistance to trying them. However, I find that if a warm and supportive climate has been developed and the facilitator is trusted, most individuals will give any exercise in this book a try. Group members need to be continually reminded that the key purposes of doing aerobics of the mind is to stretch their thinking, to get new ideas, and to try doing different things so that the neurons and dendrites in the brain are stimulated and energized.

Is there a recommended way to put these exercises together into a program so that many parts of the brain get exercised? I wish I could tell you which exercises would stimulate certain parts of the brain, but our knowledge is simply not that advanced. A recent report on brain research indicated that through the use of positron emission tomography (PET) scans, the hot colors in the scans mark the areas of the brain working on various tasks. The researchers note that speaking words, generating words, seeing words and hearing words all take place in different parts of the brain. So the research has begun, but is not far enough along for us to pinpoint exercises for different parts of the brain. For now, it's exciting just to know that new dendrites can be grown.

The best advice for developing a 60- to 90-minute program of exercises that will stimulate various parts of the brain is to pick a variety of activities from the different chapters here in Part III.

Some people like to plan around a theme. For example, if it is Christmas time and you want to acknowledge the holiday, you can pick exercises and slant them toward that theme. **Chapter 8, "Will You Be My Valentine?"** in Part II is a good example of a theme program that uses exercises from a number of different chapters in Part III and adapts them to a Valentine theme.

Be creative as you develop your programs. Use the material here, but add your own innovative ideas. And remember that your enthusiasm and excitement will be contagious.

Improving Your Memory

As stated in the **Preface,** the brain has as many as 100 billion neurons, many with 100,000 or more connections through which to send signals to neighboring neurons. Even though we lose some neurons as we grow older, these neurons can sprout new dendrites and synapses late into life and thereby form new connections with one another. Research is beginning to show that stimulating and challenging the brain increases its capacity to stay vital and healthy and to retain and enhance memory.

In spite of this exciting new knowledge, the concerns and anxieties about forgetfulness are rampant. People still believe that serious memory loss is a normal part of aging and that "you can't teach an old dog new tricks." It is an everyday occurrence to hear stories of what someone has lost, of the difficulty remembering names, of the inability to remember what was read. Some of these stories are funny; some are sad. All have an element of frustration.

This chapter is based on the assumption that memory changes do occur as people age, but that nearly everyone's memory skills can be improved with practice and training unless there is some impairment of the brain. These aerobics-of-the-mind exercises are intended to help people improve their attitudes about their memories and stimulate memory improvement.

Factors that may affect memory

When considering memory it is important that participants give some thought to factors that may affect the memory process.

Give the members of the group this list of items that are generally accepted as factors that may affect memory:

◈ Problems with attention

◈ Negative expectations

◈ Stress

◈ Anxiety

◈ Depression

◈ Loss and grief

◈ Inactivity

◈ Lack of organization in daily life

◈ Fatigue

◈ Some physical illnesses

◈ Some medications

◈ Vision and hearing problems

◈ Alcohol

◈ Poor nutrition[1]

Ask the participants to check those items that may have been factors in their experiences of forgetting. Ask them to recall times when their memories seemed to be especially bad and encourage them to think about what might have caused that. Ask them if they can recall times when their memories seemed to be unusually sharp and to reflect on why that might have been. Involve them in a discussion so their awareness is raised about factors that can affect memory. (See **Appendix C** for materials that will enhance your knowledge about factors that may affect memory.)

Brainstorming ways to improve your memory

Begin the session by saying something like this:

> People who have studied memory have suggested
> many things to do to improve memory. Many of us have
> developed our own tricks to improve our memory so
> instead of letting "the authorities" tell us how to do it, let's
> do some brainstorming and list the many ways we have
> devised to help ourselves remember. Brainstorming will
> help us think of things we already do, but then it will press
> us to think of new ways to sharpen our memories.

This would be a good time to review the rules of brainstorming found in **Chapter 10, "Creative Problem Solving."**

Begin the brainstorming process by focusing on a specific problem:

> You've lost your car keys again. You had them yesterday.
> Now you've looked high and low and can't find them.
> What can you do to avoid this irritating problem?

The group members will undoubtedly generate ideas such as:

◈ Always put them in the same place.

◈ Say out loud where you are putting your keys.

◈ Attach a bright colored ball of yarn to the keys to make them more visible.

Be sure to continue to press for ideas even after the group members think they have run out of ideas. This is when new and creative ideas are likely to emerge.

After brainstorming about lost keys, move on to brainstorm about how to remember other things that members may have lost. Encourage them to share their experiences in losing things and then have them focus on a specific incident and brainstorm about it. For example, someone may have carefully hidden money that was to be used for a special purpose and now he or she can't find it.

Remembering what you read

Give the participants a story to read. Ask them to concentrate as they read and to make a decided effort to remember what they are reading. Point out that we often read with no intention of remembering. Tell them that they will be asked several questions after they have had time to read the story several times. A story such as "The Small Cage Habit" (next page) can be the focus.

After the group members have read the story, ask these questions:

1. What kind of bear is the story about?
2. How many steps did the bear make as she paced back and forth in the cage?
3. Who decided to build a new space for the bear?
4. Who gave a speech at the celebration?
5. Where was the band from that played at the event?
6. What adjective is used to describe the bear?

This is a simple story followed by easy questions. Most participants will do well.

Now try a newspaper article such as "Long-term Care" (page 80). (You may want to use an article from your local newspaper.) This article by Tom Frazier, Executive Director of the Coalition on Aging Groups (CWAG) in Wisconsin appeared in the Summer 1995 issue of the *CWAG Advocate* and focuses on long-term care of older people.

Follow the reading of the article with at least five questions related to the article. After the questions, allow time for discussion of this important issue.

Again point out that concentrating on what you are reading and making a deliberate effort to remember makes a difference.

The Small Cage Habit

Once upon a time there was a very sad polar bear who was kept in a very small cage in the town zoo. When the sad bear wasn't eating or sleeping, she occupied her time pacing . . . eight paces forward and eight paces back again. Again and again she paced the parameters of her very small cage.

One day the zookeeper said: "It's depressing to see this bear pacing back and forth in her confining cage. I shall build her a great open and elegant space so that she may romp with great freedom and abandon." And so he did.

As the space was completed, great waves of excitement charged through the town, and finally the magic day came to move the bear to her new headquarters. The town mayor delivered a rousing speech, with a chorus of children screaming in anticipation.

The city marching band manifested a brassy bravado of sound that reached a crescendo at the glorious moment that the sad bear was ushered into her elegant new quarters. Whispers of curious expectation rose from the crowd as they watched the great beast frozen in the uncertainty of the moment. The sad bear looked to her left and to her right, and then she began to move . . . one step, two, five, eight paces forward and eight back again . . . again and again. To the shocked amazement of the crowd, she still paced the parameters of her old very small cage.[2]

Long-Term Care

I have come to believe that state legislators and government leaders are not ready to face the reality that community care must be as viable an option as institutional (nursing home) care.

The arguments are simple and compelling. First, the fiscal argument. Home and community care costs the state less money overall. If people can be served in their own homes and communities instead of having to go into nursing homes it will cost taxpayers less. Wisconsin's premiere home care program—the Community Options Program (COP)—makes it possible for people needing long-term care to stay at home. Part of the beauty of the program is its flexibility. It allows people needing care at home to get the services they need to keep them there. The tragedy is that we have allowed 8,300 people to sit on waiting lists to be served. The wait is more than five years in some counties. For a majority that wait is too long, and many end up going into a nursing home anyway at taxpayer expense or they die. The cost to taxpayers is much higher for nursing home care on average than it is for community care. Fiscally, it makes sense to keep people at home.

Secondly, people overwhelmingly prefer to remain in their own homes. Just ask them. The possibility of having to go to a nursing home is distressing to anyone needing long-term care but particularly to those who do not need that level of care. For someone who just needs assistance with cooking a meal and taking medications but who has no money or resources to get these services, going into a nursing home is not the common sense option. But that is what is happening to people who need help because there is no waiting list for nursing home care—if you qualify, you get it—whether it is the best option or not. Socially, it makes sense to keep people at home.

Sketching and diagramming to remember

Some of us were taught diagramming as a way to learn sentence construction. It was a carefully prescribed system, but the idea of diagramming can also be used as a tool to remember what we read. Ask the participants to read a short article and then reduce the article to a sketch with some diagramming and words. Discourage note taking that uses words only. The idea is to sketch and write a few words in a shorthand sort of way that will reinforce the memory. Researchers tell us that words and visual images reinforce each other.

Each person will do this exercise differently. Some will have difficulty thinking in this visual way. Assure them that there is no one right way to do this and that it is good mental exercise to try.

The "Identifying Bald Eagles" information (page 82), which was taken from a leaflet developed by the Ferry Bluff Eagle Council of Sauk City, Wisconsin, can be used for this exercise.

Identifying Bald Eagles

It is difficult to mistake an adult bald eagle for any other bird, because of its distinctive white head and tail and its immense six- to eight-foot wingspan. But immature bald eagles aren't so easy to distinguish, because they don't acquire the snow white head and tail feathers until they're four to five years old. Immature bald eagles have varying amounts of white mottling all over, often with distinct white patches in their "underwing pits." First year birds tend to be quite dark. The amount of white in their coloring increases each year, until they become the gorgeous adult birds we're all familiar with.

Bald eagles weigh from 8 to 14 pounds. Male and female birds look alike, except females are larger. Eagles spend the majority of their time perched in trees, conserving their energy. Only about two percent of their time is spent flying and feeding. Eagles can live to be 20–30 years old. Their eyes are six to eight times better than human eyes. They can fly at 50–60 mph, but can reach up to 120 mph in a dive.

After the participants have read the information, ask them to draw a sketch and diagram, using pictures and a few words. Now ask them to answer questions related to the article. Encourage them to discuss whether or not this exercise facilitated their remembering facts from the article.

Here is an illustration of one person's sketch and diagram of this information.

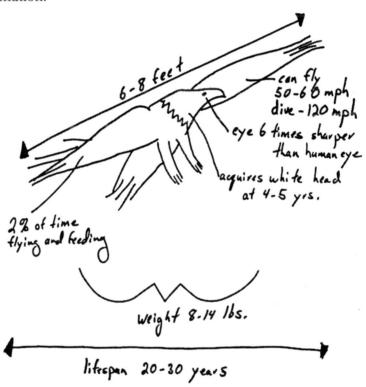

Remembering names

Remembering names of people we have just met is a challenge
for most of us. Here are several ideas that will foster better
name memory.

Explain to the participants that creating an association with a
person's name often helps to remember the name. One technique
is to link the person's name with some physical characteristic of the
person. For example, the name Betty Gill could be remembered in
this way: Visualize a fish with large gills (Gill) that is playing a betting
(Betty) game with another fish. Or the name Helen Walrack might be
visualized as a walrus (Walrack) hell (Helen) bent on swimming fast.

Another technique is to associate the person's name with something
familiar to you. For example, the name Mary Shepherd might be
remembered using the nursery rhyme, "Mary Had a Little Lamb,"
and visualizing this Mary shepherding her lambs.

To develop skills with these two memory techniques have each
member of the group develop an association for his or her own
name. Ask each to share these associations with the group.

Then suggest that each person pick the names of three different
people in the group and develop associations using either
characteristics of the person or some other association that comes
to mind. Again have them share their creations with the group and
be prepared for lots of laughter.

Giving a meaningless list meaning

Often we need to remember a list of words or letters that are not
especially meaningful in themselves. How can we remember them?

If the participants learned music, they may have learned the names
of the treble spaces by remembering F-A-C-E, and the names
of the treble lines by remembering Every Good Boy Does Fine.
This technique takes the first letter of the item to be remembered
and forms it into either a new word or a new sentence. Ask the

participants if they have other things they remember with the use of this technique.

Now let's say we want to remember the colors of the rainbow, which are violet, indigo, blue, green, yellow, orange and red. Write the names of these colors on the chalkboard and ask the participants to devise a way to remember them by forming a new word or a new sentence.

Next list on the chalkboard the names of the planets: Mercury, Venus, Mars, Jupiter, Saturn, Uranus, Neptune and Pluto. Ask the group members to form a new word or come up with a sentence that will help them remember these names.

Realizing that not everybody is just dying to remember the colors of the rainbow or even the planets, let's be practical and work on a grocery list. Let's assume you need milk, bread, pickles, soup, apples, crackers, carrots and salt. Ask the group members to invent a way to remember this list using this technique.

If there is time, ask the participants to suggest lists they would like help remembering and have the group members put on their creative hats. Maybe someone needs to remember the names of her 11 grandchildren or the names of the streets in her neighborhood.

Remembering what you see

Find a picture in a magazine or newspaper that is filled with action. Give all the participants a copy of the picture and ask them to consciously pay attention to everything portrayed, paying special attention to details. You could also use a large art print that portrays a number of actions such as a Breughel painting of village folks playing games or attending a feast, or a Seurat painting of a circus.

After the group members have had time to observe the picture carefully, ask them to cover the picture and then ask them questions such as:

◈ How many people are in the picture?

◈ How many animals or birds are in the picture?

◈ What are the people wearing?

◈ What are the people and animals doing?

◈ What does the picture mean to you?

Each picture will suggest its own set of questions.

Usually participants will be surprised at the details they have missed or forgotten. If there is time, use a second picture as a way of encouraging more active observation.

A picture in your home

Ask the participants to remember a picture that is hanging in their homes and to describe it in detail in writing. Then request that when they go home they check their description against the original. Suggest that they study the picture carefully and then report back on what they have learned. The purpose of all this is, of course, to help them sharpen their powers of observation.

Words in place of numbers

Most of us have a need to remember numbers such as our social security number, car license number, bank account number, important phone numbers and fire lane number if we live in a rural area.

We can help ourselves remember these numbers by translating them into letters or words that have meaning for us. For example, my fire lane number is W4448. I remember it by saying to myself "Walter fast, fast, fast ate." (Walter is a friend who eats fast.) Silly, but it works. My husband's license plate number is LYP 449. I remember it by recalling "Lip for 49ers."

Ask the participants to try their hand at finding words that give meaning to some number in their lives. Since most people know their phone number and their zip code, ask them to decide which numbers they would like to remember better and encourage them to be creative. Suggest that humor and exaggeration tend to reinforce our memories.

Linking to improve memory

You are going to the grocery store and want to remember to buy five items: Fish, milk, peas, bananas and soap. Instead of writing a list, you can use a method of linking these items together in your mind as a way to remember. Each item is linked to the next by visualizing the two together. However, it is important to link only two items at a time. Ask the participants to picture the fish swimming in milk, peas floating in the milk, bananas chasing the peas and a bar of soap hitting a banana on the head. Ridiculous, isn't it? The wilder the better. After reciting the above illustration ask the group members to name the five items on the grocery list.

Then ask the participants to invent their own list of six items and to develop a way of linking the items. If someone says, "Why not just write a list?" an appropriate response might be, "This way to remember stretches my brain and is a lot more fun."

Peg words

A longstanding memory device is that of remembering unrelated items in a given order. Ask the participants to learn the following ten words, each pegged to a number:

1. A bun for one
2. A shoe for two
3. A tree for three
4. A door for four
5. A hive for five
6. Sticks for six
7. Heaven for seven
8. A gate for eight

9. Wine for nine

10. A hen for ten

When the group members have learned these pegs, ask them to make up a shopping list of six items. These six items might be gas, stamps, bread, oranges, mayonnaise and light bulbs. Thus you can visualize gas being poured over a bun, stamps sticking on the outside of the shoe, bread hanging from the tree, oranges splattered over the door, a hive covered with mayonnaise, and light bulbs growing on the end of sticks.

Try it! It works!

Changing your surroundings to remember

A good way to remind yourself of a specific task to be done is to change something in your surroundings so that you notice the change. This change then serves as a reminder of what you need to do.

I have a friend who crosses the first and second finger of her right hand when I am in conversation with her as a way to remind herself of something she wants to tell me. Another friend moves a ring on her finger to the corresponding finger on the other hand as a way to jog her memory.

Ask the participants if they use changes in their environment as a way to remind themselves of something. List their ideas on the chalkboard. Ideas might include: A note on the door of the car to remind yourself to pick up the cleaning, a chair in front of the steps to remind yourself to put out the garbage, and a book in your purse to remind yourself to stop at the library.

Give the participants a sheet of paper with these memory concerns listed and ask them to think of ways to jog the memory by using changes in their surroundings:

◈ You are working in the garden and want to remember to call a friend when you finish.

◆ You are standing at the bus stop and want to remember to get your shoes repaired.

◆ You are running an errand and need to remember that you need to call your dentist.

◆ You are in the shower and want to remember to send a birthday card to a family member.

◆ You have just gone down to the basement and want to remember to put a letter out for the mail carrier.

◆ You have gone for a walk and want to remember that you need to start the washer when you get home.

◆ You are on the phone with a friend and need to remember that the iron needs to be unplugged.

More exercises

There are many excellent books about improving your memory. See Appendix C for titles and authors.

Creative Problem Solving

In this day of nuclear fusion, the Internet and space stations, our world is changing very rapidly. The discoveries and innovations of the next 20 years will make changes in the previous 100 years seem snail paced.

We cannot foresee exactly what knowledge we will need five or ten years from now to meet life's problems. We can, however, develop attitudes and abilities that will help meet future challenges creatively. Developing creative problem-solving skills can be a key element in making successful personal adjustments and in developing the ability to meet new challenges.

Participants will be asked to think up ideas—their own ideas—regarding a variety of problems in need of solutions. The activities are challenging to the brain and fun.

Brainstorming

Brainstorming is a creative thinking procedure. (It is not to be confused with barnstorming or brainwashing.) It was invented by creative person Alex Osborn, founder of the Creative Education Foundation in Buffalo, New York.

Brainstorming is a simple procedure that can be used to stimulate creative thinking and problem solving. The purpose is to generate a long list of possible solutions to problems.

The main principle of brainstorming is deferred judgment, which means postponing evaluation of ideas until later. Any sort of criticism or evaluation simply interferes with the generation of imaginative ideas.

The key ground rules for brainstorming are:

1. Criticism is ruled out.
2. Freewheeling is welcomed, the wilder the better.
3. Quantity is wanted.

Real life problems that need solutions

Ask each participant to make a list of problems and challenges that are most important in their lives. Give each person a list of words that will help them think about problems and challenges in their lives. These can be listed on a piece of paper, chalkboard or flip chart.

List such words as family, friends, neighbors, church, car or transportation, social life, attitudes, finances, hobbies and leisure time, plans for the future, hopes and desires.

Ask the participants to list on a piece of paper the different problems and challenges suggested to them by these words. An alternative would be for them to do this as a group, each person voicing his or her ideas while someone writes them on the chalkboard or flip chart.

Be sure to allow a good stretch of time for participants to identify problems and challenges in their lives.

When all ideas seem to be exhausted, ask the group members to pick one problem or challenge that they would like to brainstorm about. Then review the above rules for brainstorming. Write the problem so all can see, and begin the brainstorming. Remind them frequently that ideas are not to be judged. As the process evolves and the group members think they have run out of ideas, press them to generate even more possible solutions. Often it is in the later part of the exercise that the most creative ideas will be generated. Remind them that wild, crazy ideas are welcomed.

At the end of the exercise, draw a circle around the idea or ideas the group considers most helpful. Allow time to discuss these ideas.

The first time I did brainstorming with a group of older women, they listed 35 problems and challenges in their daily lives. The one they chose to brainstorm about was loneliness. What a time we had! The list of ideas developed for dealing with loneliness was awe inspiring, ending with the notion that perhaps loneliness isn't all that bad; it's what we do with it. The group was open and honest and eager to deal with this real-life issue even though it was the first time any of them had done brainstorming.

Exercise *A bus trip*

> You are taking a bus trip that will continue for three days. The bus is very crowded. You are seated next to a person of the opposite sex about your age or older who has the same destination. This person talks constantly to you and even pokes your arm if you start to doze. You have two more days of this.

Ask the participants to list as many ideas as they can for ways to deal with this problem. When they think they have finished, press them to generate even more ideas. Remind them often to defer judgment. At the end, ask them to indicate the idea or ideas they like best.

Exercise *Pet peeves*

Everyone has pet peeves; for example, people who smack their gum or people who phone you and can't stop talking. Ask each participant to name one pet peeve. List them so that all can see. Then ask the group members to pick one pet peeve for everyone to brainstorm about. As indicated previously, this may be done individually or as a group.

When the group members have chosen one, ask them to list all the ideas they can dream up to reduce this irritation. Tell them to have fun listing all kinds of ideas, zany as well as sane ones. And to be sure to defer judgment.

Ask them to set a goal, such as 20 ideas or more. Then encourage them to try for ideas to meet their goal.

Exercise   *Attainment of a goal*

Ask participants to indicate on a piece of paper one goal that they would like to attain within a month. Then ask them to list a minimum of 20 ways to help attain the goal.

At the end of the exercise, ask if members are willing to share what they have written. Assure them that it is all right to keep their goal and solutions confidential if they choose. Many will be willing to share, and that will make for a positive experience for everyone.

Follow up on the goal

Follow up within several weeks by asking participants to share their progress on achieving the goal. Plan a time for discussing their experiences in achieving the goal. At the end of the month ask how many have achieved their goal.

As you can readily perceive, creative problem solving and brainstorming, in particular, are not just exercises that last for a short time. The ideas that are born can have value in the lives of the participants.

More brainstorming ideas

Assuming that you have found brainstorming to be a wonderful way to stretch the mind and have fun at the same time, here are additional ideas that can be used in brainstorming sessions:

◆ Be sure to use ideas generated in previous sessions such as Real Life Problems That Need Solutions. Usually many problems and challenges surface and provide rich topics for future brainstorming sessions.

◆ What can you do when time after time the doctor keeps you waiting?

◆ What can you do when your husband is around the house all the time and it's driving you crazy?

◆ What can you do when telephone solicitation calls interrupt your meals, television viewing or other activities?

◆ What can you do to stop worrying?

◆ What can you do when someone makes a rude remark to you?

◆ What can you do when a friend is always late and it creates problems for you?

◆ Your children give you a gift that you can't use and yet you don't want to offend them. What to do?

◆ You have just retired and have moved to a new home after living in the same place for 35 years. What are some ways to adjust to a new environment?

◆ You can't drive at night but want to continue to go out for dinner, to programs and meetings. What can you do?

◆ We tend to celebrate 50th wedding anniversaries by having an open house or a dinner party for family and friends. What other ways could we celebrate 50th anniversaries?

◆ The little book *Random Acts of Kindness,* by the editors of Conari Press, tells brief stories of people who gave unexpected gifts to others or performed acts of kindness that were out of the ordinary. Ask group members to read stories from the book. Then ask them to recall acts of kindness they have experienced. Brainstorm about random acts of kindness that could be carried out by members of the group.

◆ Night after night you have trouble going to sleep. List as many new and creative ways you can think of to help you go to sleep.

As you have realized by now, these are just a few of many problems and challenges that can be dealt with through brainstorming. The possibilities are endless.

Product improvement

Brainstorming can also be used as a way to improve a product. The following examples will give you ideas about how to develop exercises that stimulate participants to think new thoughts:

◆ Boots are often a problem. Besides being difficult to get on and off, they have zippers that break, heels that run over, colors that are drab and finishes that get dull. What ways can you think of to improve on boots?

◆ You have several mice in your house and want to get rid of them. Mouse traps have never worked very well for you. Think of as many ways as possible to improve on the mousetrap.

◆ Your grandchild has a stuffed chicken toy. He or she likes to drag it around, but doesn't seem to enjoy playing with it. Think of as many ways as possible to change this toy so that it would be more fun for play.

◆ You like having a cup of tea, but are often irritated at how fast the tea gets cold. How many ways can you think of to keep the tea hot to the last drop?

◆ You live alone and would like to continue to mow your lawn. The mower, however, is very heavy to push, is hard to move up the inclines in your yard, and makes a loud noise that hurts your ears. Think of as many ways as possible to improve on the lawn mower.

◆ You have trouble getting dresses on over your head because of your arthritis. List a number of ways to redesign dresses that would make it easier to get dressed.

As you have guessed, the sky's the limit on the kinds of problems that can be dealt with through brainstorming product improvements. You might ask the participants to come up with their own list of ideas to brainstorm about. Remember that brainstorming is an excellent way to stimulate the neurons and dendrites in the brain.

New uses for brainstorming

Brainstorming can be useful in developing new uses for objects:

◈ You have a sack full of empty wooden spools in your closet that you have saved for years, thinking that someday you will do something with them. List as many new uses for these spools as you can.

◈ Many of us now recycle metal cans, but they have hundreds of interesting and unusual uses. List as many uses for these cans as you can, not limiting yourself to one size. You may use as many cans as you wish.

◈ The common lead pencil is always with us. How many new uses for pencils can you list? You may use any size pencil and as many pencils as you like.

◈ Sometimes we find it difficult to throw away cardboard boxes. There are hundreds of interesting and unusual uses for these boxes. Use any size and as many as you like and see how long a list of possible new uses you can generate.

◈ The common paper clip is usually used to hold papers together. Think of at least 30 new ways to use paper clips.

◈ The world is full of discarded tires. Think of new uses for old tires.

The possibilities for brainstorming about new uses for common or discarded items are endless. Have fun thinking of new ones.

Lists for fluent thinking

Challenging your memory to make long lists can be stimulating and fun. This can be done individually using paper and pencil, or as a group activity using the chalkboard:

◈ Ask the participants to list as many birds as they can. Before beginning ask the group members to guess the number of birds they think they can list. Usually the group members will totally underestimate the number they can recall. They will be pleasantly surprised and pleased with themselves at the number they can list.

◈ List as many kinds of trees as you can.

◈ Name as many vegetables as you can. Try listing fruits as well.

◈ Name as many wild flowers as you can.

◈ List the songs you remember singing when you were a child (or songs from the '40s, '50s or '60s).

◈ List all the animals you can think of that walk on four legs.

◈ List the names of as many American Indian tribes as you can. (There are several hundred of them. This exercise might send participants to their encyclopedias to check out their lack of knowledge.)

Imagination and a dot

Put a chalk dot on the blackboard. Ask the participants, "What is it?" Take some time and encourage the group members to use their imaginations. Answers may include such things as a fly speck, a bird in the sky, a spot on a dress, a seed, a period, a small button, a speck of dust in your eye. One person who tried this exercise with children got 87 ideas in three minutes!

Stimulating Discussions

A challenging discussion can help build a stronger and healthier mind. A stimulating discussion is a learning experience, a valuable social activity and often fun.

But all of us have been in discussion groups that haven't gone smoothly. Inevitably participants wander from the subject; often one or two people dominate the discussion; sometimes everyone talks at once.

These guidelines are offered as suggestions to facilitate the process. The leader:

◈ Sits in the circle with the participants.

◈ Sets the stage and defines clearly what the focus of the discussion will be.

◈ Encourages everyone to feel free to participate, but no one is forced to speak if he or she chooses to be silent.

◈ Indicates at the very beginning that if someone talks too much or dominates the group, the leader will interrupt and make sure others have an opportunity to talk.

◈ Guides the group members in staying "on track."

◈ Informs the group that silence and gaps in conversation are normal and a healthy part of a good discussion.

◈ Explains that disagreement is expected and accepted, but participants are expected to respect the opinions of others.

If the leader sets forth these guidelines at the beginning of a discussion, the chances for a profitable and happy time are greatly enhanced.

A short version of these Ground Rules for Discussion, used at the White House Conference on Aging in May 1995, are listed on the next page. They could be printed on cards and given to each person as a reminder at the beginning of a discussion session.

A discussion on wisdom

Here are suggestions for facilitating a discussion on a characteristic that most older adults have developed through the years. The discussion should help participants appreciate and value their wisdom and thus enhance their self-esteem.

To begin the discussion, ask the participants to:

◈ Define what they understand by the concept of wisdom.

◈ Tell what they think constitutes a wise person.

◈ Think about the wisdom they have. When do they feel the wisest?

◈ Identify the most important thing they have learned about living.

The ideas generated can be written on a chalkboard or flip chart as the discussion progresses.

The discussion might be summarized by writing a free-verse poem using the ideas generated by the group. A free-verse poem simply lists, with an economy of words, the essence of the ideas generated.

Favorite saying

Ask the participants if they have a favorite motivational or inspirational saying to share with the class. It can be something that the participants say over and over again to themselves, perhaps out loud, which helps them cope with challenging experiences in their lives. It could be something from the Bible, a poem, a saying from a famous person or something they have made up on their own. Most of us have such words of wisdom tucked away, but seldom talk about them with others. This can be a special time of discussion and sharing.

Ground Rules for Discussion

◆ Each person's opinion counts.

◆ Everyone participates—no one dominates.

◆ One speaks; others listen.

◆ It's okay to disagree, but not to be disagreeable.

◆ Speak positively.

◆ Stay focused.

What is your dream for the future?

Arthur Fleming, a former head of Social Security in our federal government, is quoted as saying when he was 90 years of age, "We must value our memories, but we must also have a dream." (See **Chapter 5, "Have a Dream,"** for more of the quote.)

◆ What is your dream for *your* future?

◆ What is your dream for the *community* in which you live?

◆ What is your dream for our *country?*

◆ What is your dream for the *world?*

Encourage the participants not to be satisfied with broad general ideas, but to think very specifically about these dreams. For example, if there is a dream for world peace, ask that they talk about specific countries where peace does not exist.

Moving into the future

Many of us feel stuck in old ways of doing things that may no longer be appropriate. But it seems to be increasingly difficult to change and move on. The goal of this discussion is to use the insights of the past to think about how we may want to adjust our attitudes and activities to be more in keeping with our present situation. Begin the discussion with these ideas or similar ones:

◆ What stereotypes of old people did you see in magazines and newspapers when you were growing up?

◆ What stereotypes do you see in the media now?

◆ Who were the people and what were the events that most influenced the paths you have taken in your life?

◆ What was your mother (father) like when she (he) was the age you are now? In what ways are you like her (him)? What do you do now that is different? What do you do that is similar? What has changed?

◆ Who in your life has encouraged you to take risks, expand your horizons?

◆ Who are your role models now?

◆ What sort of role model are you?

◆ How would you like to be remembered when you die?

◈ If a newspaper reporter were to write about you ten years from now, what would you want him or her to say?[1]

Ask yourself if it might be wise to set new goals and plans for the future while you still have choices.

What do you value in your life today?

Ask the group members to write down five things they value most in their lives right now. Suggest that they first take some time to think about their values and to write them on a piece of paper. Then ask the participants to share those they feel comfortable sharing and have someone write those on a chalkboard or flip chart. It will be interesting to see how many values are similar or dissimilar.

Then ask the group members to pick one value they treasure most and tell the others why. Allow for as much discussion as possible, encouraging individuals to talk about their values as much as they feel comfortable.

Possible values:

◈ To have a good relationship with my children.

◈ To have a number of friends and acquaintances.

◈ To be able to come and go as I choose.

◈ To have the freedom to do the things I want to do.

◈ To have good health.

◈ To live in a place that is secure and safe.

◈ To have enough money to live comfortably.

◈ To have a satisfying spiritual life.

◈ To feel loved and be able to give love.

Technology and values

In our lifetime we have seen many new technologies developed. Let's list as many of these new developments as we can, for example, telephone, telegraph, airplane, refrigerator, electric washer and dryer, television, computer, VCR, telephone answering machine. This could be a very long list, and participants can be pressed to think of as many as possible.

Then ask the participants to review this list and discuss the following questions:

◈ Which ones would you not want to live without and why?

◈ Which ones could you live without and why?

◈ How have these new technologies affected our values?

Being reckless and foolish

Tell the participants that radio show host Garrison Keillor once said, "As we get older we're supposed to get more reckless and foolish." What do you think he meant?

If you were going to do something reckless and foolish, what would it be? It might be something you've always wanted to do. The discussion might then lead into whether or not doing that now is possible.

The animal you would like to be

Chose the animal (or bird) you would like to be. Then tell why. Chose the animal (or bird) you would least like to be. Then tell why.

This makes for a lighthearted discussion. Expect gales of laughter.

This exercise can be varied by substituting for animals and birds such things as flowers, toys, colors, sounds, musical instruments or smells.

Discussion topics to stimulate the imagination

The possibilities of discussion topics are endless. The following topics are designed to stretch the imagination and stimulate new and creative ideas. Some participants may find these topics quite ridiculous, but with encouragement the hesitancy and reservations that may exist at first blush will vanish. You probably would not use more than one or two of these topics in any one session:

◈ What would you do if someone gave you a barrel of pickles?

◈ What would you do if someone gave you an Arabian horse?

◈ If someone gave you a million dollars, what would you do with it?

◈ If you were free to do whatever you wanted to do, what would that be?

◈ If you were to be cast on a deserted island, who would you want to be with?

◈ If you were able, what would you like to clean up, fix up, paint up?

◈ What is your idea of an ideal vacation?

◈ If you were reincarnated, who would you like to be?

◈ If you could create something very beautiful for the world, what would it be?

◈ If you were to make a movie, what would it be about?

◈ What would you like to invent? What would it do?

◈ If you could choose a different name, what would it be? Why would you choose this name?

◈ What do you think of when you look at the moon?

◈ If you could invite a famous person to come to your group, whom would you invite?[2]

Discussion topics that encourage reflection

◈ What is there about yourself that makes you laugh or smile when you think about it?

◈ What is it that makes you feel the most happy?

◈ What are some new activities that you would like to try?

◈ What do you fear most about growing older?

◈ When you think about death, what comes to mind?

◈ What is it that makes you feel the most angry?

◈ What kinds of things do you do when you feel lonely?

◈ What is your most valuable treasure?

◈ What is one of your favorite ways to express love to someone?

◈ What makes you cry?

◈ What are some things you used to be afraid of but are not anymore?

◈ Name several people you admire and tell why.

◈ What is the funniest thing that ever happened to you?

◈ What are some things you have achieved in your life?

◈ What are some things you would like to learn?

◈ How could you treat yourself better?

◈ What are some things that give you peace of mind?

◈ What are the easiest ways for you to learn something new?

What if

This series of questions pushes creative thinking to its limits.
Encourage the participants to be freewheeling and flippant.
Assure them that no idea is too crazy.

◈ What if we had no cars?

◈ What if we could understand the sounds (language) of the birds?

◈ What if clouds had strings attached that hung down to the earth?

◈ If the moon could talk, what would it say?

◆ What if animals were more intelligent than people?

◆ What if we lived to be 200 years old?

◆ What if we never had to sleep?

◆ What would happen in the world if water did not freeze?

◆ What if the earth were shrouded in fog and all you could see of people was their feet?

It would be a wonderful exercise for a group to generate its own "what if" questions.

Completing sentences

Give the participants a piece of paper with these incomplete sentences on it. Be sure to leave plenty of room between the lines for them to write in their responses.

◆ People will think of me as . . .

◆ I miss . . .

◆ The thing I like about myself is . . .

◆ I would like to be . . .

◆ It is fun to . . .

◆ Five years from now, I . . .

If the group members are willing, ask them to share what they have written and to discuss their ideas.

Many questions

Ask the participants to write the answers to these questions as they are read. At the end of the questions the group members can share answers and discuss their choices.

◆ What food do you like best?

◆ What is the most interesting television show?

◆ What is the best movie you have ever seen?

◆ What is the most timesaving home appliance?

◆ What is the most interesting trip you have ever taken?

◆ Who is the most influential woman or man in your lifetime?

◆ What song do you most enjoy?

◆ What is the best book you have ever read?

◆ What animal would you most like for a pet?

◆ What is the most important influence in your life?

◆ What would you most like to do in the next year?

◆ What is the best joke you have ever heard?

Right Brain Exercises

Thishis chapter provides ideas for encouraging creativity in the visual arts through nonthreatening paper and pencil exercises.

Usually someone in a group will say, "I can't even draw a straight line." A good response is, "Drawing straight lines is often a hindrance." Another will say, "I never was any good at art." The facilitator can assure the group members that aerobics-of-the-mind exercises aim to stimulate many parts of the brain, but artistic skill is not expected.

Going for a walk with a line

Each person will need a piece of white shelf paper at least 22 inches long or two pieces of 8$^1/_2$-by-11-inch paper taped together end to end plus a set of crayons. Ask the participants to sketch or draw what comes to mind as you read the story of a young Swiss girl named Heidi (page 110). It works best to begin at the left-hand edge of the paper. At the end of the exercise the participants may choose whether to share what they have sketched.

Heidi

Heidi lives in the Swiss Alps. One morning she decides to go for a hike. Her dog, Wolf Wolf, tags along with her.

At first they follow a winding path in the foothills through a field of colorful spring flowers. Soon they cross over a fast-flowing stream. The sun is warm on Heidi's face and arms.

Wolf Wolf wags his tail as they begin to climb upward through the trees. A clump of shrubs hides a small bunny.

The climb is becoming more and more steep. A very large mountain looms ahead.

Suddenly there appears on the path in front of them a mountain goat. As Heidi and her dog continue to climb, several large birds fly overhead.

Two big boulders challenge their climbing skills. After awhile they come upon a small hut on the side of the mountain.

Heidi is beginning to feel hungry and tired so she takes out the lunch she has packed for herself and Wolf Wolf. They eat until their stomachs are pleasantly full.

The sun is very warm. A tired young girl and her dog curl up and take a nap.

If the group members like this exercise, suggest that they compose one or more of their own stories and then follow the above procedures to sketch the story.

Floor plans of your childhood home

Tell the participants to draw a floor plan of the house where they lived as a child, indicating the location of the doors and windows. Ask them to sketch in the furniture as they remember it. The participants may or may not share what they have drawn. If they do share, you probably need to limit the time for each person to talk to two to three minutes. This is an exercise that generates much discussion.

After the floor plan is finished, ask the participants to write a paragraph about some memorable event that took place in that house.

An alternative idea is to draw a floor plan of the kitchen they remember best from their childhood and then tell something that happened in that kitchen.

Finish the line drawings

The facilitator develops a format, such as the one shown on page 112, by drawing lines on an $8^1/_2$-by-11-inch piece of paper so that it is divided into six equal sections. Then the facilitator draws a few lines or shapes in each section that will challenge the participants to add to those lines and make a realistic picture. It's a good idea to give each participant at least two copies of the format so that after doing the exercise once they can try it again, developing even more creative ideas.

A recent event in your life

Tell the participants to draw or sketch a scene from a recent event in their lives. Suggest that they keep it simple, using a few lines to sketch the action. Encourage them to share their pictures and to tell

Finish the line drawings.

others about the event. Newsprint and pencil work well, but $8^1/_2$-by-11-inch paper and crayons or colored pencils can also be used. Remind the group members that there is no expectation of fine drawing skills but that this exercise is designed to challenge the brain.

Doodling

Tell the participants to take a piece of paper and a pencil and begin to doodle, letting their minds wander, trying not to think about what they are doing but just letting the ideas flow.

After a few minutes ask the participants to look at their doodles. What have they drawn? What does it look like? What could it have been? Turn the paper at different angles and observe what is there.

Ask the participants to exchange papers with the person sitting next to them. The neighbor should write down how many different things he or she sees in the doodling. Then return the paper to the owner.

Discuss with the participants any difficulties they have had in being free to do the doodling and in using their imaginations in interpreting what they drew.

Assure the group members that this exercise may seem frivolous but has a sound purpose in helping them be more imaginative and creative. Affirm that doodling can make their dendrites grow.[1]

Shared doodling

Give each participant paper and pencil. Ask each person to make a doodle or a scribble on his or her piece of paper. Each then passes his or her paper to the next person, who adds more doodles. The paper is passed again, each trying to make a picture from the doodles. Lines are connected or other features are added. The point is to do as little as possible to the doodles to make them look like something.

Designing your own dinner plate

Give each participant a piece of paper with a large circle drawn on it. Ask each person to imagine that the circle represents a dinner plate and to take the opportunity to design his or her very own plate to be used by him or her alone. The goal is to strive for imaginative and creative designs.

Making designs with scraps of paper

Have available construction paper in a variety of colors. Ask the participants to pick one piece of paper and tear it into various sizes and shapes. Encourage them to make some small pieces and some larger pieces. When each has torn up a sheet of paper, ask that all the pieces be placed in the middle of the table and mixed together.

Ask each person to choose about six or eight pieces of paper and arrange them into a form that suggests a bird or other animal. Then using a whole piece of construction paper and rubber cement or other glue, ask each person to paste down his or her creation.

The last step is to give the "work of art" a title.

Tear-out artistry

Supply each participant with a piece of construction paper. Have the group members hold the paper behind their backs and try to tear out the shape of a pig, cow or any animal they may choose. For special holidays you could select an item such as a Christmas tree, Valentine or Easter rabbit. Collect finished works of art and let everyone join in appreciating each other's work. This is a lot of fun!

Finding designs with yarn

Make available a dozen balls of yarn of many colors. If participants are knitters or weavers, they can be asked to bring several balls of yarn. Give each participant an $8^{1}/_{2}$-by-11-inch piece of white paper. Ask each person to develop a design by draping the yarn on the paper. Encourage the participants to experiment with various colors and lengths of yarn, pushing the material this way and that until they come up with a design that is pleasing to them. Rubber cement or other glue can be used in fastening the design to the paper. If gluing proves too difficult, assure them that the value of the exercise is in doing it, not in preserving it.

Finding a design with scissors

Give each participant an $8^1/_2$-by-11-inch piece of white paper, a pencil and a pair of scissors. Ask that each person trace around the scissors. Now ask the participants to try to change this outline of a pair of scissors into something completely different, turning the paper any way they choose. Suggest that they give their creation a name or title.

A picture takes the place of a word

Ask the participants to write a short letter to a friend using paper and pencil and substituting a picture for a word throughout the letter. Several examples:

I love Wisconsin cheese.

Nobody knows how much I pine for you, dear.

Nursery rhymes lend themselves to this activity. Try "Hi diddle diddle, the cat and the fiddle, the cow jumped over the moon. The little dog laughed to see such a sight and the dish ran away with the spoon."

Draw what you hear

Play a recording of a piece of music. Ask each person to draw a picture of what he or she hears. Try a variety of music such as a waltz, a polka, a favorite hymn, a folk song or songs familiar to everyone such as "Jingle Bells," "Over the River and Through the Woods" and "Pop Goes the Weasel." Indicate that the picture does not have to be a realistic one, but can simply be lines and colors that express feelings.

Ask the group members to discuss what they heard and what they drew.

Drawing with straight lines

Ask each person to draw a picture using rulers and pencils and no more than 12 straight lines. The lines may be of any length the artist chooses, but they must be straight. Many drawings can come out of straight lines: trees, roads, buildings, trucks, trains, furniture, people.

Writing exercise

Give each of the participants one piece of paper and two pencils. Ask them to pick up both pencils and write their names with both hands at once. Then ask them to write their first names with their left hands and their last names with the right hands, both at the same time. To stretch the brain even further, ask the participants to hold the paper against their foreheads and write their last names.

Timeline

Give each person a piece of paper with a timeline drawn on it. The timeline is created using a piece of $8^1/_2$-by-11-inch paper and drawing a straight line the length of the paper with a ruler. Divide up the line with small vertical marks indicating 10, 20, 30, 40, 50, 60, 70, 80 and 90 years. Tell the participants that this is a timeline representing their lives. Ask them to write in happenings and events that fill them with pride and joy and a sense of fulfillment. If they are so inclined they could sketch small pictures rather than using words.

Lines revealing emotion

Using felt-tip pens and white paper or newsprint, draw a cluster of lines that may change from one feeling into an opposite. Be sure to let the lines themselves express the idea and not represent specific objects:

◆ Draw nervous lines changing to relaxed lines. For example:

◆ Draw bold lines changing to delicate lines.

◆ Draw tired lines changing to active lines.

◆ Draw angry lines changing to calm lines.

◆ Draw tortured lines changing to free lines.

◆ Draw crude or awkward lines changing to graceful lines.

Lines of sounds and touch

Lines can express sounds we hear and things we touch.

◆ Draw lines that express the bangs of fireworks.
   For example:

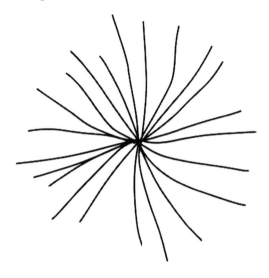

◆ Draw lines that express vibrating noise.

◆ Draw lines that express crinkly.

◆ Draw lines that express prickly.

◆ Draw lines that express aching.

◆ Draw lines that express smooth.

◆ Draw lines that express hard.

◆ Draw lines that express scaly.

Lines can express an idea:

◆ Draw flowing and foaming water.

◆ Draw rocks and flowing water.

◆ Draw flat land and distant plateaus.

◆ Draw rolling hills and distant mountains.[2]

Designs from circles

Ask each person to cut ten circles of equal size (about four inches in diameter) from black construction paper. Each circle is to be cut up according to different instructions and rearranged to form a related whole:

1. Cut a circle apart in the middle.

2. Cut a circle apart so that one-fourth is separate.

3. Cut a circle apart with an **S**-shaped cut. For example:

4. Cut a circle apart with two cuts forming an **X**.

5. Starting from one edge, cut into the circle to form rays of the sun.

6. Starting from the center, cut into the circle to form rays of the sun.

7. Starting from one edge, cut the circle apart with four curvy lines.

8. Continue cutting up the last three circles using your own ideas.

If the participants wish, they can glue down their designs on white paper to preserve them. Usually people are surprised at how much fun this is and what interesting designs they can produce.[3]

Ink blot art

Fold a sheet of paper in the center. Put a drop or two of ink in the fold and then press the fold together. Unfold it and observe the unique shape that has been formed. Ask the participants to try to explain what the design represents.

A story picture

Develop a story using pictures cut from magazines. Also cut words or letters of the alphabet from the magazines. Arrange on a sheet of paper into a collage that tells a story. Give the story a title. Urge the participants to be as free and imaginative as possible, assuring them that no idea is "too crazy."

Your hidden self

Ask the participants to look through magazines and find pictures of items that represent their "hidden self." Explain that this hidden self might include hopes and dreams they ordinarily do not talk about. Ask them to think about their secret wishes and desires.

If this exercise seems too threatening, an alternative could be to find pictures in magazines that represent their "real self," that is, the self others see and know about. This could include representations of their families, their homes and their special interests.

Quilt designs

Have available newsprint cut into 12-inch squares and a pair of scissors for each participant. Begin by asking each person to fold the square on the diagonal so that a large triangle is formed. Then fold this triangle again so that a smaller triangle is formed. Fold this triangle one more time. Holding the longer fold toward the body, begin cutting on the outside corner. When each person has progressed a little way with the design, ask the participants to turn the other folded edge toward their body and work out the second motif, which may be a repetition of the main figure. Provide enough 12-inch squares so that each participant may have at least five different tries at making a design for a quilt.

Art Appreciation

Many older people have not had the opportunity to become acquainted with works of art, to go to art galleries, to learn about the lives of artists and to become familiar with different styles and modes of art.

This chapter describes ways to introduce older people to a few of the paintings of those considered outstanding artists. In a way it is a beginning art appreciation course.

Most older participants can readily respond to realistic paintings; abstract art is more of a challenge. When I first began taking art prints to a senior center and dared to show them artists such as Rouault and Miró, they quickly confessed, "We don't like that kind of art." I suggested we look at it briefly and raise some questions about it as a challenge to stimulate our brains. They smiled and "went along with the teacher," eventually becoming quite adept at analyzing "modern art." We agreed that most of the art prints we studied would not find a place in our homes.

What to look for in works of art

Place a large print (most are 21 by 28 inches) of a painting so that all can see it easily.

Write the list of things to look for (page 123) on a chalkboard or large sheet of paper for all to see.

Introduce the picture by telling its title and something about the artist who created it. Brief facts about prominent artists can be found in an encyclopedia or on the Internet.

Ask the group members to respond to the previous questions while looking at the picture. You will find that most participants respond readily and can easily participate in a lively discussion.

Alternative approaches

Help the characters come alive

Some prints lend themselves to an approach different from consideration of the previous questions. If there are people or animals in the picture, ask each participant to pick a person or animal and give it a name. Then ask that the participants write a few sentences about the person or animal. Encourage them to be imaginative and creative. Ask that they share what they have written. I have been amazed at how inventive and full of good humor this approach can be.

Sunday Afternoon on the Island of Grande Jatte by Georges Seurat lends itself to this exercise.

Working in pairs

For maximum mental stimulation, give every two people a small print (11 by 14 inches or smaller) and a page with the **What to Look for in Works of Art** questions (next page). After working with the questions, the team might also choose to write a story about the picture.

What To Look for in Works of Art

◆ What kind of lines do you see?

◆ What shapes can you find in the picture?

◆ What colors has the artist used?

◆ Point out the textures found in the picture.

◆ What mood or feelings do you think the artist was trying to create?

◆ What thoughts come to mind as you look at this picture?

What is happening in the picture?

If the picture is one filled with action, the following exercises can be used:

◆ Write out all of the questions you can think of about the picture. Ask the questions you would need to ask to know what is happening. (The facilitator should encourage the participants to generate as many questions as they possibly can.)

◆ Write as many possible causes as you can of the action shown in the picture. You may use ideas of what might have happened just before the events depicted in the picture. Or you may list ideas of what happened a long time ago that made these things happen.

◆ List as many possibilities as you can for what might happen as a result of what is taking place in the picture. Wild guesses are acceptable.

Pieter Brueghel the Elder's paintings such as *Children's Games* lend themselves to this exercise.

Where to get prints

I find most of the prints I use at a local shop whose business focuses on selling prints. However, many libraries have prints that can be checked out. Usually they are framed, which is a nice plus.

The National Gallery of Art in Washington, DC, is a rich resource. You may order their Color Reproductions Catalogue to view the wide variety of art prints available. The gallery will mail 11-by-14-inch prints (see **Appendix C**).

Some of the art prints I have used are actually posters, designed by personnel at art galleries or museums to advertise their exhibits.

Slides can also be used in these exercises. Slides of famous art works are often available from local libraries.

If copies of works of art are not readily available to you, try asking participants if they have a painting they would be willing to bring for group analysis and discussion.

The following are works of art I have found useful:

◆ *Sunday Afternoon on the Island of Grande Jatte* by Georges Seurat
◆ *The Circus* by Georges Seurat
◆ *Children's Games* by Pieter Brueghel the Elder.
◆ *Peaceable Kingdom* by Edward Hicks
◆ *American Gothic* by Grant Wood
◆ *Piano Players and Checker Players* by Henri Matisse
◆ *Goldfish* by Henri Matisse
◆ *Three Musicians* by Pablo Picasso
◆ *Mother and Child* by Pablo Picasso
◆ *People and Dog in the Sun* by Joan Miró

◆ *Starry Night* by Vincent Van Gogh

◆ *Washerwoman* by Auguste Renior

◆ *The Sacrament of the Last Supper* by Salvador Dali

◆ *Les Plumes en Fleus* by Marc Chagall

The possibilities for using the visual arts in aerobics-of-the-mind exercises are endless.

Once the participants get the hang of what to look for and how to approach a work of art, they will be delighted with themselves and with you for introducing them to this vast source of mental stimulation.

Fun with Optical Illusions

Optical illusions activate the imagination and intellect of the viewer. As we view illusions, tilt them on their sides, turn them on their heads and squint our eyes to get a different perspective, we find ourselves stimulated, amazed and delighted.

Most people are intrigued by optical illusions and find them fascinating. Some are "one time" illusions. Once you have seen it, you've "got it." Other illusions elude you over and over again. Illusions fool us; they convince us of things that may not be true.

Only a few illusions are presented here. But my hope is that facilitators and participants will be motivated to seek out other sources such as *Can You Believe Your Eyes?* by J. Richard Block and Harold Yuker (see **Appendix C**), which contains 250 illustrations that facilitate playing with illusions and contributing to dendrite growth. See **Appendix B** for some tips regarding these illustrations.

What do you see first? What else do you see?
Can you see both at once?

What do you see? Can you see the old woman?
Can you see the young woman?

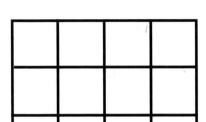

How many squares do you see? Continue to look
and see if you can find more squares?

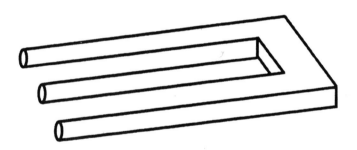

How many prongs does this object have?
Look at it another way. How does it change?
Cover up the three circles on the
left-hand side and see what happens.

How many cubes are there in all? How many cubes are entirely hidden and cannot be seen?

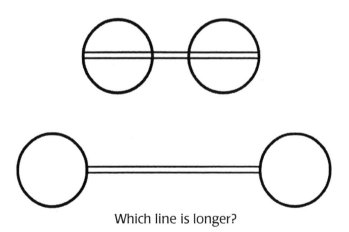

Which line is longer?

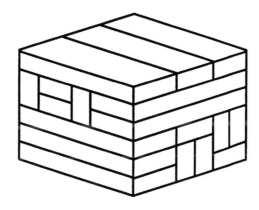

How many pieces of wood are necessary
to form the cube shown here
if all the pieces are the same size?

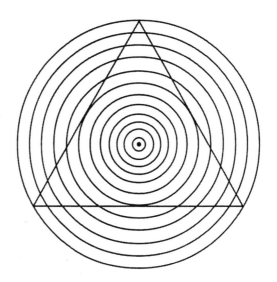

Are the sides of the triangle straight or curved?
If the lines seem curved, are they bent
inward (concave) or outward (convex)?

Which numbers do you see? Try to add
these numbers. What would the total be?

What do you see in these figures?
Now that you see them both,
can your attention alternate between the two?[1]

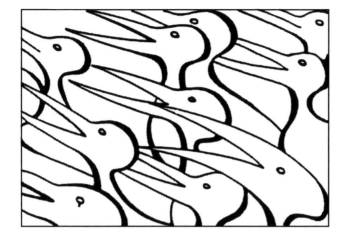

Is the figure in the lower right
of each picture a bird or an antelope?[2]

What do you see in this figure?

What do you see in this figure?

What do you see in this drawing?[3]

Sharpening the Senses

The world is a wonderful place. There are so many treasures to experience—to see, hear, taste, smell and touch. We often take these riches for granted. Our senses seem to be dulled by years of living. Sometimes we say, "I've seen it all" or "I've heard it all." But have we? Or do we need to sharpen our senses to see the sunset anew, listen to the birds again, savor the soup we eat, sniff the lilacs once more and enjoy the feel of a kitten's fur? Making conscious efforts to be more aware can bring much joy to our lives.

This chapter provides exercises that will remind the participants of how we often take our senses for granted. The activities encourage increasing the power of the senses. The emphasis is on paying attention, focusing and practicing.

The chapter is divided into four sections: **Seeing, Hearing, Smelling and Tasting** and **Touching.**

SEEING

Vision is by far our most important sensory channel. Some researchers say approximately 90 percent of the information our brains receive comes through the eyes. Yet we often look without really seeing. Looking is a generalized viewing; seeing is a keen visual awareness.

Observing it all

Ask the participants to look around the room in which they are meeting. Ask them to list on a piece of paper every object they see, from the largest item to the smallest detail. Give this exercise plenty of time, encouraging group members to not just look, but really see.

Most people are amazed at the long list they will generate and will admit that many items on their list are usually unnoticed.

Alphabet observation

In this exercise of observation, the first person names an object in the room that begins with *A,* the second person names an object that begins with *B,* and so on with the letters of the alphabet until everyone has had a turn. (Participant's names, clothing, jewelry and other personal items may be used since they are in the room.) Using invisible items such as air, heat and moisture will add more intrigue to the game.

The egg

Sketching an object is an excellent way to sharpen the visual senses. Many participants will hesitate to sketch or draw, but they can be encouraged to try by indicating that the purpose is not how to duplicate the image exactly, but to sharpen their ability to see.

A good object to start with is an ordinary egg. As participants try their hand at sketching a simple egg, they will be amazed at the new appreciation they gain for the subtle and beautiful shape of an egg. If some people are discouraged with their ability to do this, do not prolong the exercise but continue to emphasize that they are learning to *really* see.

A teacup can offer another opportunity to sharpen the visual senses through observation and sketching. As participants express their concern about their drawing abilities, reassure them that their brain cells are responding to their efforts.

What's in your hand?

Have the participants look at one of their hands. Ask them to look at the palm and trace with their finger the lines and furrows. Feel the texture of the skin. Is it soft, rough, dry, moist? Feel the flesh that cushions the bones. Feel the bones under the skin and flesh. Observe the veins on the back of the hand. Check out the fingernails. What shape are they? Are there moons at the base of the nails?

Ask the participants to place one hand flat on a sheet of paper and trace around it with a pencil. Notice if the fingers are short or long. Notice if the hand is long and slender or short and boxy.

To increase awareness, ask the members to compare the outlines of their hands with those of their neighbors. How does it look in terms of width, length and special bumps?

If there is a bulletin board or blank wall available, post the drawings of the hand and observe the differences. It will increase awareness of how alike we are, and yet how different?

Observing ourselves

Divide the group members into pairs.

Ask the participants to look carefully at their partners for two minutes. Suggest that they observe carefully every detail of their partners' appearance, such as hair, clothing, jewelry and shoes. Then ask that they turn their backs on each other and change three things in their appearance.

Now ask the partners to face each other and try to discern what changes the others have made in their appearance.

This can be great fun, especially if partners make subtle changes such as rebuttoning a blouse or lacing their shoe strings differently. Encourage them to be "tricky."

Observation of trees

If it is possible, take the group members outside so they can observe trees. First ask the participants to name the trees they see. Then ask them to observe the different shapes of the trees and discuss what they notice. Suggest that they look closely at the bark and indicate what differences they observe. Ask if they see any shadows and have them describe what they see. Ask them to observe the distance between the trees.

This exercise can be enhanced if it is possible for them to do a rubbing of the bark of a tree. Regular typing or duplicating paper and the side of a crayon can be used.

Observation of a picture

Ask the participants to bring to the group session a picture of their mother or someone else they know or have known well.

Ask them to turn it upside down. Study the nose, the ears, the mouth. Point out that they will probably notice things about her they have never noticed before.

Tell the members of the group that these new observations come because they are seeing the person in a new perspective—upside down. They may notice other characteristics that otherwise tend to get lost in an all-too-familar face.[1]

What do we miss seeing?

As a way to raise awareness of how often we look but do not really see, ask the following questions:

◈ What color is the upholstery in your car?

◈ Which coin—a penny, nickel, dime or quarter—has a building on it?

◈ What color is the lining of your purse or wallet?

◆ What color was the sky when you got up this morning?

◆ What brand name is on your toothpaste tube?

◆ What kinds of wood are used in the furniture in your living room?

◆ What color are the door knobs in your home?

◆ What is the design on the stamps you are using now?

◆ Describe the face of the person who delivers your mail.

Now ask the participants to devise their own list of questions and take turns asking each other.

Thinking in images

Share information about guided imagery with the participants. Tell them that guided imagery is consciously created visualization. For example, a golfer who wants to improve her game will practice hitting the ball over and over again. Research shows that if the player consciously visualizes in her mind the best possible stroke, the visualization will actually help improve her game. This kind of guided imagery, called *mutual rehearsal,* has been used by Olympic teams around the world.

Explain that we can use this technique of guided imagery to improve some of our activities. Perhaps there are swimmers in the group who want to learn to do a new stroke or to swim farther than they usually do. Suggest that they create a visualization in their minds that incorporates a new goal. Or perhaps there are members who go to exercise class but have trouble doing a certain exercise. Suggest that they practice the exercise in their minds, doing it over and over again, and then note if their ability to do the exercise the next time improves.

This may seem far fetched to some participants, but if they are willing they can pick a goal and try the visualization exercise. It can work and can be a big surprise to those who have not tried it previously.

HEARING

In today's world we are constantly bombarded with sounds and noises from radio, television, automobiles, airplanes and crowded rooms. It seems there is no one single sound to hear and more often no silence. Often in self-defense we tune out. If our hearing is not quite as good as it used to be, we find the accumulation of sounds disturbing.

In this section participants will strive to recover sensitivity to individual sounds and develop anew an appreciation for those sounds.

The sounds around us

Ask the participants to be very quiet and observe the sounds they hear. Is the heating system humming? Is a dog barking? Is the wind blowing? Are heating ducts creaking? Are windows rattling? Are dishes clattering in the kitchen? Is someone talking in the next room? Is a television playing?

After three minutes, ask each participant to write down what he or she heard and then share it with the group members.

Hearing the sounds of nature

If possible take the participants out into a quiet woods. Ask that they listen to the rustle of leaves, the song of the birds, the flow of water, the sounds of animals. Ask that they make a list of the sounds they hear.

If it is not possible to go to the woods or a park, play a tape or CD of nature and bird or animal sounds. There are many on the market now. Ask that the group members close their eyes and listen to the tape and then write what they hear.

Identifying sounds

Make a tape recording of sounds commonly heard around the house. These might include the tick of a clock, the sound of the furnace, the flushing of a toilet, the banging of pans in the kitchen, an electric mixer or blender, the garbage disposal, a door slamming, a rocking chair creaking, the door bell ringing, the click of a light switch, someone typing on a typewriter or computer, water running in the bathtub, a hair dryer blowing, a piano playing, the television blaring and the refrigerator humming.

Ask the group members to try to identify each sound and write it down. Then compare answers.

Ask the group members to talk about the sound of silence. Is there such a thing? Do they like silence or is it disturbing? If they like silence, where do they go where it is quiet? If they dislike silence, what sounds do they like most?

How are you?

Blindfold one of the participants and silently designate another person to ask, "How are you?" The blindfolded person tries to guess who spoke. If she cannot guess, ask the designated person to say a few more words. Continue to take turns blindfolding group members and designating others to speak. Take time to discuss the reasons we might have trouble identifying a person's voice when we cannot see him.

Exercise in hearing

Bring to the group a variety of objects that make sounds. These might include a music box, a toy train whistle, a spoon and bowl, a cow bell, jingle bells, beans to pour into a bowl, a Halloween rattle, a balloon to deflate, sandpaper and a piece of wood, a saw and a piece of wood, dry leaves, a deck of cards to shuffle, dice to roll, and different kinds of paper to rustle such as tissue paper, brown wrapping paper and newspaper. This exercise is limited only by the leader's imagination.

The leader should make these sounds out of sight, perhaps just asking group members to turn their backs. The participants will list on paper the sounds they can identify. The group members can compare their findings at the conclusion of the sounds.

Soothing sounds, irritating sounds

Ask the participants to list ten sounds that are very soothing to them. Next ask the group members to list ten sounds that are very irritating to them.

Spend some time discussing these responses. Ask them to reflect on experiences that may have influenced how they feel about certain sounds.

SMELLING AND TASTING

Sometimes as we get older we say our ability to smell isn't as good as it used to be. But a recent report of a survey on smell done by *National Geographic* magazine indicates that "Aging does not bring a uniform decline in 'smellability.'"[2] A good question is, "Does the sense of smell actually decline, or do we fail to pay attention and to train ourselves to make it better?"

In this section are exercises that can help sharpen our sense of smell and taste, two closely related senses.

Smell the fruit

Divide the participants into groups of four. For each group provide half an orange, half a grapefruit, half a lemon and half a lime. Ask the participants to take turns closing their eyes while another person holds the four fruits for them to smell. The object is to identify which fruit is being smelled.

Other items to smell and distinguish between might be sage, oregano, basil and bay leaf. Another combination of seasonings might be cinnamon, nutmeg, cloves and ginger. There are many other possible combinations. Four is not a magic number—perhaps six or eight spices could be smelled at one sitting.

Smells in the sacks

Put together a series of small paper lunch sacks (5 by 11 inches is a good size), each of which contains an item with a distinct smell. These items might include an onion, a bar of soap, a tea bag of mint, a piece of lemon, a few cloves, pine needles, a small jar of Vicks VapoRub®, perfume, sharp cheese, a piece of turnip or a sachet. If it is spring, any number of aromatic flowers could be used. If it is fall, items like dried leaves or a walnut still in its hull would be good choices.

Number each sack and ask participants to make a list of numbers—one for each sack—on a sheet of paper. Pass the sacks to each person, asking participants not to look inside. As the sacks come around, each person is to write what he thinks is in the sack.

After everyone has had a chance to smell each sack, ask for responses. Some will find that when they cannot see what they are smelling, identifying the smell eludes them. This is fertile ground for a discussion of why this is so.

Describing what we smell

It is not easy, but describing in words what we smell helps to sensitize us to what we smell. It is a good exercise in bringing together our sense of smell with the words we use. Ask that the participants try to find one or two adjectives to describe each item.

Describe in words the smell of each of the following:

◆ Rain
◆ Burning leaves
◆ Onions frying
◆ Cabbage cooking
◆ Sour milk

◆ A wet dog

◆ Freshly mown hay

◆ Freshly cultivated soil

◆ A sweating body

◆ Gasoline

◆ Dirty hair

◆ A rose

Ask the participants to read what they have written.

Follow this exercise by asking the group members to devise their own list of distinct smells to be described in words.

Smells and memories

Ask the group members to talk about their memories related to particular smells. What memories are associated, for instance, with each of the 12 items listed in the previous exercise?

Or the discussion could be more open so that each participant remembers an experience that happened in the previous week which can be associated with a smell. This exercise is an effort to bring present day experiences into play instead of always looking back into the past.

Apple time

During apple season buy several different kinds of apples for a taste test. Begin by comparing color, shape, size and skin of the apples. Then cut small pieces of each apple for the participants to taste. Ask them to keep notes on each. See if the participants can identify each apple by its taste.

Teatime

Brew up at least five different kinds of tea. Using small paper cups for sampling, ask the participants to try to identify the kind of tea and also to describe the taste.

TOUCHING

The sense of touch has been largely underdeveloped in our culture. This may be a result of too many no-nos as we were growing up such as "don't touch—it might break" or "don't touch—it's dirty" or "don't touch—that's naughty."

With some effort it is possible to recapture what we naturally had as children—the desire to touch and to enjoy the feel of things. This section focuses on activities that can help us sharpen our sense of touch.

Touch without looking

In numbered paper lunch sacks place articles to be touched but not seen. Ask each person to list numbers from 1 to 12 on a piece of paper. As the sacks are passed around the room the participants are to feel what is in the sacks and then write the names of the objects.

Objects that can be used include a piece of fur, pine cone, can opener, gourd, yarn, small brush, coins, buttons, coffee beans, pencil, safety pin and sand. Let your imagination be your guide in picking the objects. If they are willing, the participants can be responsible for setting up the exercise.

Some participants may find they have difficulty identifying objects when they cannot see them. If this occurs, take advantage of this discovery to encourage a discussion of why this is so.

Describe without naming

A variation on the previous activity is to ask the participants to feel the objects in the sacks, but to refrain from naming them. Instead ask them to write a description of the objects. In many ways it is more of a challenge to the brain to describe the objects than to name them.

The touch of nature

Take the participants outside into a garden or woods. Divide the group into pairs. One person in each pair will be blindfolded first and will be led by the other to touch different objects. These objects might be the trunk of a tree, a rock on the ground, the leaves of a plant, the petals of a flower, the soil, lichen growing on a tree, a bush with berries, or water in a stream or pool.

When one person in the pair has had the experience, the other person is blindfolded and led to the various objects.

This can be an eye-opening experience since we usually see things in nature but don't focus on touching them. When the group members come inside, have them discuss the experience.

The bread of life

This exercise combines four of the five senses: Seeing, smelling, tasting and touching. (I'm not sure there is a way to hear bread, but I may be missing something.)

Provide a piece of bread for each participant. I prefer to use a homemade bread with heavy texture, but any light white bread could be used as well.

The participants are asked to look at the bread, smell it, taste it, touch it in a deliberate and thoughtful way and then write what they have experienced.

◈ What does it look like? Color? Texture?

◈ What is the smell?

◈ What is the taste?

◈ How does it feel?

◈ Why is bread often referred to as "the staff of life"?

Feeling is believing

The participants sit in a circle with their hands behind them. One member of the group moves around the circle and puts a different object in each pair of hands. Then each person is asked to identify what is in her hands.

There is no end to possible objects to use, but here are a few ideas:

◈ Spool of thread

◈ Eraser

◈ CD

◈ Tea ball

◈ Nail

◈ Small wooden car

◈ Wind-up toy

◈ Card from a deck of playing cards

◈ Fold-up fan

If the participants are familiar with sewing, you might use small pieces of different kinds of cloth such as wool, cotton, silk, linen, brocade, velvet, net, suede cloth, lace and eyelet. Tailor this activity to your group and, if possible, ask for help choosing the objects.

Games Make Brains

G ames have fostered aerobics-of-the-mind exercises for both children and adults in generation after generation. I remember my mother planning and leading games for her friends at potluck dinners, club meetings and parties when I was a young child. She knew instinctively that games were valuable mental stimulation and, of course, fun.

This chapter presents games that seem to me to be of particular interest to able, older adults. I have chosen not to include throwing and catching games, hopping and jumping games, pulling and pushing games, or hiding or racing games, although with some groups these might be appropriate (see **Appendix C** for ideas). The games in this chapter focus on activities that stimulate the mind, although some movement and action are included.

My tendency in facilitating games is to minimize competition. I try to avoid the winner/loser mentality, and I do not give prizes or awards. Often one or more people need some encouragement and help from other group members or the leader in playing a game. That is perfectly acceptable and indeed is part of the total process.

You may recognize many of these games as ones we played in our childhood and youth. You will no doubt think of games not included here. I have chosen ones that have worked well in my experience. Many other games that focus on words are included in **Chapter 17, "Words, Words, Words."** These games will quicken the mind, spark new energy and tickle the ribs.

Cap, mitten, rattle

Divide the players into two teams. If the group sits around a table, indicate a dividing line in the middle. With two sets of cap, mitten and rattle, have the first person on each team begin by putting on the cap and mitten and shaking the rattle. Then the person takes off the cap and mitten, shakes the rattle and passes all three items to the next person. Each person in turn puts on the hat and mitten and then shakes the rattle. In the process of everyone's participation you can expect a lot of joviality. The team that finishes first wins, but winning is really irrelevant. Use your imagination about the rattle. It could be a baby rattle, a Halloween noise maker or an egg beater.

I give you a cat

The players sit in a circle or around a table. The following questions and answers are used:

> The first player says to the second: "I give you a cat."
>
> The second player responds: "A what?"
>
> The first player then says: "A cat"
>
> The second player turns to the third person with: "I give you a cat."
>
> The third player responds: "A what?"
>
> The second player responds: "A cat."

As soon as the first player is finished speaking to the right-hand neighbor, she turns to the left-hand neighbor and says: "I give you a dog." The cat and the dog are relayed around the circle and when they meet, that player must keep them straight and keep the conversation going. Eventually the cat and the dog will arrive back where they started. If you want to be especially creative, try substituting animals such as tiger and lion, cow and horse, gorilla and baboon or anything else.

Rhythm

The players sit in a circle or around a table. Ask all the players to follow your motions to establish a rhythmic movement. Pat both hands on your knees (or on the table) twice, clap your hands twice, snap the fingers of your right hand and then snap the fingers of your left hand. (It doesn't matter if the snap is silent; it's the motion that counts.) Have the players practice the motions and rhythms a number of times until they have them clearly in mind.

The game begins with the leader starting the rhythm and everyone joining in. On the right-hand snap, the leader says "rhythm" and continues without losing a beat. On the following right-hand snap, the leader calls out any letter he chooses to the player on his right. This player then gives a word beginning with that letter as the rhythm is continued. The next player calls out a letter and the person next to him responds with a word beginning with that letter. And so on around the circle. If someone misses a beat or a letter or a word, simply begin the rhythm again.

This game is a gentle challenge to coordination of mind and body. Once the players catch on (this might take a session or two), it may become a favorite.

Buzz

The players are seated in a circle or around a table. One player starts the game by saying "one," the next player "two," and so on around the circle until the number six is reached. Then the word "buzz" is substituted for the word seven.

The players continue counting, each time substituting "buzz" for any number in which the digit 7 occurs, such as 27, 37, 70. "Buzz" is also substituted for any number that is a multiple of 7 such as 14 and 21. Upon reaching 70 the response is "buzz-one," "buzz-two," and so forth. the number 77 is "buzz-buzz."

When a player says "buzz" at the wrong time, or says a number when "buzz" is called for, that player drops out of the game. The game continues until all are out.

Animal, bird or fish

The players sit in a circle. The lead player says, "Animal, bird or fish?" and points at one of the players. The leader then repeats one of the designations such as "fish" and counts to ten.

The person pointed to must respond by giving the name of a fish before the count of ten is reached. The leader then repeats, "Animal, bird or fish?" and this time may say "animal" and again counts to ten.

If a player is unable to respond with an answer, she becomes the leader and has a turn at challenging other group members.

Twenty questions

Players sit in a circle or around a table. One person is asked to leave the room. While this person is absent, the group agrees on a person, animal or object. The "outside" player is asked to return and then begins asking questions that can be answered only by "yes" or "no." The goal is for the person to guess what the group has in mind by asking only 20 questions or less. It is helpful to narrow the possibilities by asking such questions as "Is it animal?" or "Is it vegetable?" or "Is it mineral?" Whether or not the person asking the questions succeeds or fails, another person is chosen to leave the room for the next round.

Recognition

One player hums, whistles or uses an instrument to play a few bars of a familiar turn. The other players write down the name of the tune. Each player can take a turn humming, whistling or playing, or one person can be the "musician" for all of the tunes. After a dozen or more tunes are presented, the players check to see who has the most correct answers.

Wise sayings

The players sit in a circle or around a table, each with paper and pencil. Each player is asked to compose a wise saying using the letters of the name of the person on his right and to write it down. For example, the name *Brown* would require words beginning with the letters *B, r, o, w* and *n*. The wise saying might be something like "Bashful relatives often win nothing." (I'm sure the players can do at least that well.)

When the wise sayings are completed, each player passes his on to the right-hand neighbor, who then reads the results.

A group story

The players sit around a table, and each is asked to write her name at the top of an 8½-by-11-inch piece of paper. Each person is asked to write down the first sentence of a story. The next move is to fold down the paper so the sentence cannot be seen, and then the paper is passed on to the person to the right. This person is asked to add another sentence to the story, in turn folding down the paper so that no writing is evident and passing it on. And so it goes around the circle until all have added a sentence to everyone's story.

Now it is time to read the disconnected stories and have some good laughs.

My mother keeps a florist shop

This is a spin of the old game "My Father Keeps a Grocery Store." The players sit in a circle. One begins by saying, "My mother keeps a florist shop, and in it she sells. . . ." The person gives only the first letter of the item, and then the group members call out what they think the object might be. For example, the person might call out the letter *g* for geraniums. The first person to guess correctly is the next to take the lead. Encourage the group members to come up with unusual, catchy varieties.

The states of the United States

The players sit around a table with paper and pencil and list the numbers 1 to 50. A map of the United States is placed on the wall or chalkboard. The players write down all 50 names of the states that make up the United States. It works best if the map is large enough to see the outlines of the states, but not so large that they can be read.

This exercise often surprises the players with its difficulty since they remember learning the names of the states when they were children. This is not a timed exercise. The players are given plenty of time. When all seem to have stretched their minds as much as possible, ask a member of the group to read off the names of all the states so the players can check their lists.

The cities of the United States

The players sit in a circle. One person begins by naming a city, for example, Chicago. The next player names a city beginning with *O*, the last letter of Chicago. The response might be Oklahoma City. No city may be used more than once.

Anyone who has difficulty naming a city can get help from a neighbor. The idea is to stretch the mind and get the neurons activated, not to see who can *win*. The game continues until the group members seem to have had enough.

Charades

The players are divided into two groups. Each group chooses the title of a book, song, movie or television program. Group 1 chooses a player from Group 2 and gives that person the title in writing, which she is to act in pantomime so that her group can guess what it is.

At the beginning of the pantomime, the actor indicates through motions to Group 2 whether the title is from a book, song, movie or television program. Any signals are acceptable but some suggestions are:

◈ Book—pretend to hold a book in your hands.

◈ Song—open your mouth as if singing.

◈ Movie—move your hands around each other as if rolling something.

◈ Television program—pretend to hold a remote control in your hand and press the buttons.

The group members may want to make up their own signals.

The actor indicates through raised fingers how many words are in the title. Then the acting begins. Words may be pantomimed individually or as groups of words, whatever is judged to be the best way to communicate. The actor refrains from speaking during the process. Before going on to the next word or group of words, the actor makes a sweeping motion to indicate the end of that idea.

When the actor has finished all the words or phrases in the title, Group 2 begins to guess what the title may be. When a guess is getting close, the actor gives a signal of encouragement; when a guess is far removed, the actor gives a gesture of discouragement.

The actor may be asked to repeat motions or to do it a different way. The goal is to enlighten group members so that they may guess the right answer. After Group 2 has guessed the title or has given up, Group 1 has its turn.

Board games

Many board games are mentally challenging. An alternative to a "regular" activity period is to set up card tables with a different board game at each and let participants choose the game they would like to play. Appropriate games would be:

◈ Parcheesi
◈ Scrabble
◈ Scattergories
◈ Checkers
◈ Chinese checkers
◈ Chess
◈ Monopoly

Card games

Card games such as bridge, sheepshead, five hundred, canasta, hearts, pinochle, rummy and euchre are fine mental stimulation. The participants may not have played these card games for years so it would be advisable to have available the rules or an informed person who can get the games started and help with questions.

Words, Words, Words

There is good evidence now that using words in different ways is a challenging stimulation for the brain. The feature article, "Quiet Miracles of the Brain,"[1] in the June 1995 *National Geographic* magazine indicates that a different area of the brain lights up when speaking, generating, seeing or hearing words. We can say with assurance that word activities are one of the richest resources for stimulating the mind.

There are hundreds of activities related to words. Entire books are written about word games. You will want to look at some of these listed in **Appendix C.**

Included here are a variety of activities with words that I have found to be of interest to older adults. They include spelling bees; tongue twisters; games like teakettle, dictionary, and scrambled words; and story and poetry writing. Many of these activities with words will be familiar. Some you will recognize as variations on games you played when you were a child.

Spelling bees

The spelling bees of school days were oral exercises with two teams, the teacher giving each person words to spell. If the student spelled the words wrong, he or she had to sit down.

This is a spelling bee with a difference since there is only one team and competition is eliminated. The participants sit around a table with each person having a pencil and a sheet of paper numbered from 1 to 20, or whatever the number of words you choose to use.

The leader pronounces each word slowly, often repeating it several times, and the participants write it down. When all the words have been given, the members of the group take turns spelling them in the order in which they were given so that each player can check his spelling.

You might ask how many missed one word, two words and so forth, but remember that competitive feelings are to be kept at a minimum. The purpose is to stimulate each mind to its maximum capacity, and that will be different for each person.

Words can be chosen at random from a newspaper, book or dictionary. You may want to choose words related to a theme. For example, I once used words related to water. These included:

aqueduct	environment
artesian	forest
bottled	ground water
canoe	irrigate
cascade	pollution
Colorado River	recycling
conservation	reservoir
desert	shower
drainage ditch	sprinkler
drought	water

The trick is to use words that are challenging to spell, but not too difficult so as to be discouraging.

Word definitions

A variation on the spelling bee is for each person to write the words that are pronounced, but also to write the definition of each. Definitions need not be dictionary-like, but should clearly define the word.

Spelling words backwards

Another variation on the spelling bee is to follow the original practice of spelling the words out loud, then immediately spelling that same word backwards. For most participants this is a good challenge. Keep the words short, at least in the beginning.

Words that go together

The participants are given a word list and asked to come up with words commonly paired with each other. I usually ask each person to do this on his own, since that provides optimum mental stimulation. When all are finished, the members share their answers.

It is surprising how many words in our language are "partners." Here are a few:

salt and pepper	sun and moon
sugar and cream	pencil and paper
milk and cookies	cats and dogs
bacon and eggs	horse and buggy
bread and butter	Jack and Jill
cheese and crackers	David and Goliath
day and night	Romeo and Juliet
light and dark	Adam and Eve

You will think of many more.

If this exercise is too easy for your group members, instead of giving them one of the partner words, ask them to come up with as many paired words as possible, giving them several examples to get started. They may want to set a goal for a given number of partnered words they can conjure up before they begin.

Words that rhyme

The leader writes a word on the chalkboard or flip chart and asks group members to think of as many words as possible that rhyme with it. There will be some surprises when words that are spelled similarly do not always rhyme such as now and snow. Encourage the participants to listen for the rhyming.

Some good words to start with are bell, sing, ball, book and tree. After the group members have rhymed short words, try some that are longer such as folder, table, chair and phone.

Another way to use rhyming words is to have the participants sit in a circle with one person in the middle. The middle person says a four-letter word and points to someone in the circle, who is then expected to say a rhyming word before the count of ten. Of course, the count could be more or less. This is a more competitive way to rhyme words but may be appropriate for your group.

Website

A fascinating new website, www.rhymezone.com, allows you to enter a word and retrieve all the words that rhyme with it. You can also ask for antonyms, synonyms and similar sounding words, among other features. If participants use computers, it would be a stimulating exercise to look for rhyming words.

Completing words

The participants sit in a circle. The first person begins by spelling three letters of a word. The person to his right then tries to finish spelling the word. It may or may not be the same word the first player had in mind. Should the second player be unable to finish the word, the next person around the circle tries to finish it. When the word is complete, the next player starts a new word. This process continues until all have had a chance to participate, either by beginning a word or by completing a word.

Omitted vowels

Write a list of words but leave out the vowels. The list could include words such as:

1. k—tch—n
2. g—rb—g—
3. b—sk—t
4. —tm—l
5. v—n—g—r
6. p—pp—r
7. c—nn—m—n

(See **Appendix B** for the answers.)

The words with the vowels missing can be written on a chalkboard for group members to do together, or the words can be duplicated on paper so that each person has his or her own sheet. I prefer the latter since each person has a more direct challenge.

As the participants understand how this exercise works, ask them to design a new list of words without vowels for another time.

Guggenheim

This word game has been popular for many years. It has been called by various names including Guggenheim, Categories, Scattergories, and Think Ups. Ask one of the participants to be the scribe at the chalkboard or flip chart. Tell the group members that they are going to be designing a chart that will stimulate their thinking. Ask the group members to think of a five-letter word that can be written across the top of the chart, each letter heading a column. Then ask the group members to decide on six classifications of objects, which are to be written on the left-hand side of the chart. The chart would look something like the following, which includes examples of birds:

	W	**O**	**R**	**L**	**D**
Birds	*whippoorwill*	*oriole*	*robin*	*lark*	*duck*
Animals					
Flowers					
Vegetables					
Cars					
Trees					

The participants fill in as many spaces as they possibly can. When they have exhausted their ideas, they then begin to share what they have written in each of the columns. The first person shares his or her first word and all who have the same word cross it out so that only those with different words are given credit. Other players announce their first words, and whenever others have the same word, these words are crossed out and not counted. This process continues until all duplicated words are eliminated. The person with the most words left can be recognized.

This game encourages creativity and can become a favorite. Usually a new chart is developed each time the game is played.

Scrambled words

The participants are given a sheet on which all the letters of the words have been scrambled. Often the words are related to a theme such as flowers, for example:

1. pypop
2. synap
3. trase

(See **Appendix B** for the answers.)

The facilitator can make up a list of scrambled words in the beginning, but then it is valuable to ask the participants to make up their own scrambled words and to present them to the entire group for unscrambling.

I have used Valentine's Day as a focus with words such as:

1. pudCi,
2. ynadC,
3. sKis
4. orArw

(See **Appendix B** for the answers.) Note that the first letter of the word is capitalized as a clue. Some groups may not need that clue. Words associated with Halloween also can provide a focus.

Scrambled sentences

Each participant is asked to write a sentence and then to scramble the words so the sentence doesn't make sense, for example:

As one gets older, it is valuable to have a dream.

The scrambled sentence might read:

Gets a valuable it is older as one dream to have.

Each player passes her scrambled sentence on to the player to the right, whose challenge is to unscramble it. When all have done the best they can, the group members share their original unscrambled sentences.

Name the words

The group members sit facing the chalkboard. A member of the group selects a word and then draws on the chalkboard a short line to represent each letter of the word. The group members then begin guessing letters, and when they have guessed correctly the leader writes the letter in the appropriate blank. This continues until the group members have guessed all of the letters and thus have spelled the word.

If a group chooses, it can keep track of all the wrong guesses by marking them on the side of the blackboard. Over a period of time it might be interesting to see if they can reduce the number of wrong guesses.

This exercise becomes more challenging if two or three words are used. Sometimes a group may choose to use the names of those present, the names of famous people, or perhaps a proverb or common saying.

Dictionary

This is an all-time favorite of mine. It not only is challenging, but can be hilarious. A dictionary is the focus of the exercise. One member of the group chooses a word from the dictionary that he is sure no one knows the meaning of. He may want to check out his assumption by asking the group if anyone knows what the word means. If someone does know, a different word is chosen.

The keeper of the dictionary writes on his paper the actual meaning of the word while all of the other participants make up phony definitions and write those on their slips of paper. Then all of the definitions are passed to the dictionary holder, who shuffles them with the real definition and reads all of the definitions aloud, giving each definition as much credence as possible.

Going around the room, the players then try to guess which definition is the right one. After all have had a chance to guess, the dictionary keeper gives the group the correct definition.

If you feel that the group needs a warm-up to this exercise, you might choose three or four words from a dictionary, listing the correct meaning along with three false meanings. This will help the group feel creative as well as sound "dictionary-like."

Teakettle

Each participant has paper and pencil and is asked to list as many homonyms as he can. Homonyms are words that sound the same but have different spellings and meanings.

When all have come up with as many homonyms as they possibly can, ask each to share her list with the group. One participant can be asked to make a "master" list on the blackboard. There are dozen of homonyms. Here are a few to prime the pump for the group:

blue—blew	bear—bare
four—fore	week—weak
rain—rein	meet—meat
be—bee	hair—hare
beet—beat	

Now ask one person to leave the room while the remaining players decide on one set of words to be used in sentences they will devise. The absent person returns and the rest of the members begin making up sentences, but instead of using the proper word or words, they substitute the word "teakettle." For example, if the words were blue and blew, the sentence might be:

The sky was a beautiful teakettle and the breeze teakettled in my face.

Players may choose to use only one of the words in a sentence, or they may want to combine the two in one sentence. The person guessing can either listen to all of the sentences composed by the group before guessing, or guess the words as soon as possible.

Words out of words

The participants are seated around a table with paper and pencil. The leader writes a long word on the chalkboard and asks the group members to see how many words they can make out of this one. Some common words to use are names of holidays such as Christmas, Valentine's Day, Thanksgiving and Hanukkah. Other good words to use might be both first and last names of group members, the name of the town or city in which you are meeting, or the name of a favorite vacation spot.

Word quadruplets

The group members sit around a table with paper and pencil. Ask them to add one letter to each of the following words so that they can form four new words by rearranging the four letters. For example: Add *m* to tie and get time, mite, emit, item.

Good words to use are:

tie	ail
mat	men
top	ore
sea	lie
lea	Ted

Pyramid sentence

Participants should have paper and pencil. The leader explains that each person will be challenged to develop a pyramid sentence—a sentence in which each word has one more letter than the word preceding it. The sentence must be grammatically correct and must make sense. Suggest that participants initially try for at least five words and then for seven or eight words as they gain experience and confidence. Assure them that since there are few one-letter words, it's all right to begin with a two-letter word. I tried this exercise on my 71-year-old husband, Ken, and this is what he created:

He
was
gone
after
sunset

It
was
cold
since
winter
arrived
suddenly

The participants need not stop with seven words but can be encouraged to make their pyramid sentence as long as possible. The members will want to share their efforts with each other.

Stairsteps

A letter of the alphabet is chosen by the group (avoiding some difficult letters like *K, Q, X* and *Z*). This letter is used to develop stairsteps of words beginning with that letter. The stairstep sequence consists of a two-letter word, a three-letter word, a four-letter word and so on. Using the letter *B*, the stairsteps might look like this:

Be
Bet
Best
Board
Boosts
Bragged
Blunders
Bratwurst

Encourage group members to form the longest possible stairsteps.

New endings for old beginnings

The participants are seated around a table with pencil and paper in hand. Ask them to write:

> Roses are red,
> Violets are blue.

Then ask them to write a new ending for this familiar Valentine verse. My experience with this technique has been very good. The most original ending was composed by a woman in her 80s who seldom spoke in the group. Her verse was:

> Roses are red,
> Violets are blue.
> Your feet stink,
> And so do you.

After we quieted those who thought it was not a "nice verse," we cheered her efforts and watched her eyes sparkle.

Another familiar verse that lends itself to new endings is:

> Thirty days have September,
> April, June and November.

You may have heard the nonsensical ending:

> Thirty days have September,
> April, June and no wonder.
> All the rest have peanut butter,
> except Grandmother and she rides a little red tricycle.

You may want to read this one as a way of communicating that no new ending would be too ridiculous.

Other poems that could be finished differently include:

The golden rod is yellow
The corn is turning brown . . .

and

'Twas the night before Christmas
And all through the house . . .

Have fun thinking up poems that would lend themselves to
new endings.

A story from 25 words

The leader writes 25 words on the chalkboard including three or
four simple verb forms such as is, are, went and were. Other words
should include nouns, adjectives and adverbs. The participants are
asked to write a story using only these words. The story may repeat
some words, but only those included in the list.

If the first try seems too difficult, permission can be given to add
two "outside" words.

Story telling one word at a time

The goal of this exercise is to challenge the imagination by having
the group members compose a story word by word. This is done
orally. One person begins, the next person adds one word, the third
person another word, and so on. Members can decide where the
punctuation goes as the story evolves.

Encourage the members to be as creative as possible and to use
unique words as the story unfolds. This can be great fun.

Four-letter word story

The participants are asked to write a short story using only words
with four or fewer letters. Suggest that they try to write a story that

makes sense and is also entertaining. The length of the story will depend on the group members and their interests and abilities. When all have written as much as they can, ask that they share their stories.

Story telling using one object

Bring to the session a tray filled with many different objects. The objects could include:

book	hammer
camera	picture postcard
Christmas ornament	teacup
deck of cards	vase of flowers
ear of corn	whistle

The sky is the limit on what can be included.

Each participant is asked to take one object from the tray and write a story of eight or more sentences about the object. Suggest that the story be creative and funny if possible. When all seem to be finished, ask each member to share her story.

Story telling from one picture

Bring to the session a picture that will be used as a focus for telling a story. The picture might be an art print, a picture from a calendar or book of art, or a photo from the newspaper. Ask the participants to let their imagination run wild as they write a short story about the picture. Then ask the members to share their stories.

Completing a story

Read the beginning of a familiar story to the group members and ask that they individually write down a different ending to the story. Good stories to use are those that everyone remembers from childhood such as "The Three Little Pigs," "Goldilocks and the Three

Bears," "Little Red Riding Hood" and "The Little Engine That Could." Encourage creativity and wild ideas. Ask the participants to share their new story endings.

Limericks

Begin by reading several limericks to the group members to remind them of what limericks are, how the rhythm goes and how they rhyme. Point out that the first two lines have three feet of three syllables each (ta-ta-DUM). These two lines also rhyme with the fifth line. The third and fourth lines (each with only two feet) rhyme with each other. The first line ends with the name of a person or place. The last line ends with an unusual or far-fetched rhyme.

Here are several examples developed after a recent trip to the southwest:

> We arrived at Custard's Last Stand
> A hungry and wearisome band.
> We went in for eats
> And found lots of seats
> And the food and ice cream were grand.

> In Sedona the rooms were palatial
> It prompted us all to be playful.
> With scenery and sleep
> And Heartline to eat
> We ended with smiles on our facial.

> There once was a man named Stan
> Who stumbled at the Canyon Gran'.
> He smiled all the while
> And joked in good style
> An exemplary genteel man.

Tell the members of the group that they will be developing some limericks together. Ask if someone will suggest a beginning line. Then ask others to contribute ideas for the second line, the third line and so on. It will take some experimenting and playing with words to come up with something acceptable to the group. Remind them that the verse does not need to make complete sense but the rhythm and rhyming are important. If this proves difficult, consider the first try as an introduction and come back to the exercise another time.

Some participants come alive in composing limericks. If this happens they may want to share their compositions with the local press or other groups, or put them into a booklet.

A list poem

Ask the participants to write a list poem while they are seated around a table with pencil and paper. Explain that a list poem is simply listing ideas focused on a particular subject.

Possible subjects are:

◈ Good things about being over 60

◈ Good things you received from your mother, grandmother, father or grandfather

◈ Things you love to do

◈ Things you want to do

An example of a list poem is:

> I like being over 60 because I can
> Sleep as late as I like in the morning.
> Plan my day's schedule with no worry of other's needs.
> Share my life stories and people will appreciate them, most
> of the time.
> Go without my bra and nobody will notice—or care.
> Sing as loud as I like in the shower and no one will hear me.
> Stop buying coloring for my hair and just enjoy letting it
> go gray.

Encourage the participants to be honest and playful in working on their list poems.

Acrostic poem

You may want to make the above exercise more challenging by introducing the concept of an acrostic poem. An acrostic poem is one in which each line of the poem begins with a specified letter. You can use the first part of the alphabet or the letters of a chosen word such as Christmas, Thanksgiving or a word of the group's own choosing. It is nice if the word chosen and the ideas generated have a common theme.

An example of an acrostic poem is:

Summer

*S*ummer heat wraps us close.
*U*rchins play ball in the alleys.
*M*osquitoes sneak around and bite.
*M*ornings may be misty and musty.
*E*venings are punctuated with fireflies.
*R*ain washes the world within an inch of its life.

Writing headlines

Participants sit around a table with pencil and paper. The leader has a copy of a recent newspaper and selects a story to read to the group. The participants are asked to listen carefully to the story and then compose an appropriate headline. After each person has composed at least one headline, ask the group members to try for another one, this time throwing caution to the wind and creating a wilder, more humorous headline. This process can be repeated several times, pointing out that often our first ideas are not our best or most original.

Finding letters

How many *f*s are in the following paragraph?

> The necessity of training farm hands for the first
> class farms in the fatherly handling of farm livestock
> is foremost in the minds of farm owners. Since the
> forefathers of the farm owners trained the farm hands for
> first class farms in the fatherly handling of farm livestock,
> the farm owners feel they should carry on with the family
> tradition of training farm hands of first class farms in the
> fatherly handling of farm livestock because they believe it
> is the basis of good fundamental farm management.

Often we overlook the most common use of *f* in the word *of*.
(See Appendix B for answer.)

Proverbs

Develop a page in which the first few words of common proverbs
are given, with room for the participants to write the rest of
the sentence:

◆ A stitch in time saves . . .

◆ A friend in need . . .

◆ A bird in hand . . .

◆ Never put off . . .

◆ What you don't have in your head . . .

◆ You can lead a horse to water . . .

◆ The early bird . . .

◆ Early to bed . . .

◆ If at first you don't succeed . . .

◆ Don't count your chickens . . .

◆ Absence makes . . .

◈ Beauty is . . .

◈ Birds of a feather . . .

Of course, there are many more proverbs. After the group members have finished these proverbs, ask them to search their memories for at least ten more or whatever number you choose.

Another way to do an exercise with proverbs is to ask the group members to invent some of their own.

Use it or lose it

This game was invented by Alice Wealti, a member of the senior center group I know best.

Each set of three items has one or more things in common. Can you figure out what that common element is?

1. artists, automobiles, cooks
2. telephones, calendars, playing cards
3. swings, sofas, church pews
4. needles, hurricanes, potatoes
5. water, baseball players, pantyhose
6. chest colds, drunken sailors, walls
7. baskets, aprons, cupped hands
8. crawling babies, carpets, knocked-out boxers
9. pork and beans, music, discharged employees
10. flowers, kitchens, poker games
11. turkeys, pillows, braggarts' shirts
12. cameras, telescopes, spectacles
13. minks, baked potatoes, peaches
14. diamond rings, Christmas trees, frosty mornings
15. televisions, marching bands, crowing roosters

(See **Appendix B** for the answers.)

Encouraging participants to compose exercises is an excellent idea. Alice, who developed this brain stretcher, gave herself a good workout.

Momilies

Some time ago a book was published by Michele Slung called *Momilies*. It was a collection of sayings and comments that mothers are notorious for uttering. Slung's examples included:

◈ Don't run with a sucker in your mouth.

◈ I'm only doing this for your own good.

◈ The more you scratch it, the more it's going to itch.

Ask the participants to recall their own list of momilies including things they have said themselves. Encourage their creative juices by suggesting they invent some new ones appropriate for present-day situations.

Dadalies

If the group members like momilies, suggest that they recall dadalies. This is fertile ground for composing new sayings that fit our highly technological world.

Analogies

Ask the group members to think of analogies as a way to describe people. This can be either an oral or a written exercise.

The dictionary defines analogy as "resemblance in some particulars between things otherwise unlike." Some examples are:

◈ He is strong as an ox.

◈ She eats like a bird.

◈ Ted is drunk as a skunk.

◈ Laura moves like a snail.

◈ George is stubborn as a mule.

◈ Shirley flits like a hummingbird.

◈ Sue sparkles like a star.

This is a good opportunity to encourage creativity and have a heap of laughs.

Tongue twisters

Tongue twisters are sets of words that are difficult to say rapidly because of the number of similar sounds. They are an excellent challenge to the circuitry of the brain.

One way to use tongue twisters is to develop a handout with some printed tongue twisters and lead the participants in trying to say them. Begin by repeating the tongue twisters quite slowly, gradually increasing the speed until the members are articulating them as fast as they can. Keep pressing for speed since this is the best stimulation to the brain. A good one to begin with is Peter Piper, familiar to everyone:

> Peter Piper picked a peck of pickled peppers;
> A peck of pickled peppers Peter Piper picked.
> If Peter Piper picked a peck of pickled peppers,
> How many pickled peppers did Peter Piper pick?

Others that have proven challenging are:

> A big black bug bit a big black bear,
> Making the big black bear bleed blood.

> A tutor who tooted a flute,
> Tried to teach two tooters to toot.
> Said the two to the tutor,
> "Is it harder to toot,
> Or tutor two tooters to toot?"

She sells sea shells by the sea shore.

The skunk sat on a stump.
The stump thunk the skunk stunk,
The skunk thunk the stump stunk.

Fussy Francie fried frogs Friday forenoon
for five famished firemen.

Busy buzzing bumblebees buzzing busily.

The sixth sheik's sixth sheep's sick.

There are a number of books filled with tongue twisters (see **Appendix C**).

Composing tongue twisters

After a session of saying tongue twisters, ask the group members to compose some of their own. This works best in small groups where participants can bounce ideas off each other. Encourage them to be innovative and not to be overly concerned about whether the twister makes good sense.

The object is to develop sentences that use one letter over and over again as the first letter of each word. Here is an example using the letter T:

Therese talks to two turkeys taking time to trim their tails.

Or using the letter *D:*

David's dog digs dirt daily.

They can be simple or complicated, but should tend to trip up the tongue.

Other word games

Many publications are available that focus on word games (see **Appendix C**).

Puzzles and Numbers

Adding a page of numbers may be a very good way to warm up the body. Researchers at the University of Minnesota Medical School learned that when persons in an ice-cold room were chilled through and through and nothing could stop their chattering teeth, the best warmer-upper was not a cup of hot coffee, but a card brimming with rows of numbers to be added.

Have you ever been aware that when you were struggling to balance your checkbook you began to feel warm? The reason, researchers speculate, is that when you do mental calculations, your breathing slows down, and this may make you feel warmer.

As I have experimented with puzzles and numbers with older adults, I have learned that some approach the exercises with enthusiasm, but others with negative feelings. Often participants, especially women, will mutter, "I never did like arithmetic." I listen, but then encourage them to think about puzzles and numbers as a wonderful stimulation for their minds.

Connecting the dots

Give each person a sheet of paper with eight sets of nine dots on it. You may also choose to put the dots on the chalkboard and ask the participants to make eight sets of nine dots on their paper. Give these directions:

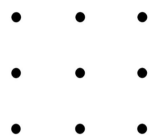

Without lifting your pencil from the paper,
draw four straight, connected lines that go through
all nine dots, but through each dot only once.

After you have tried two different ways, ask
yourself what restrictions you may have set up
for yourself in solving this problem.

Unless the members of your group have tried this puzzle before, they will struggle intensely to follow the directions. After a reasonable length of time draw the answer on the chalkboard (see **Appendix B**).

Follow with a group discussion of why we tend to restrict ourselves to staying within the perceived box.

Moving coins

Arrange ten coins to make a triangle. (I usually bring in my penny bag. You may want to ask each participant to bring ten pennies with them.) Give these directions:

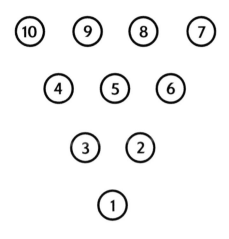

By moving only three coins,
turn the triangle upside down.

(See **Appendix B** for one solution.)

Triangles

Ask the participants to count the number of triangles found in this drawing. It may be helpful for members to number the small areas and then write down the combinations that make up all the different triangles (see **Appendix B** for the answer).

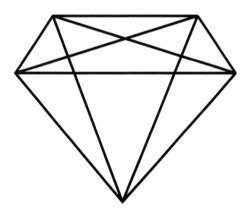

Matchsticks

Ask the participants to arrange nine matchsticks in a triangle as indicated here. Then ask them to rearrange five of the matchsticks so there are a total of five triangles (see **Appendix B** for one answer).

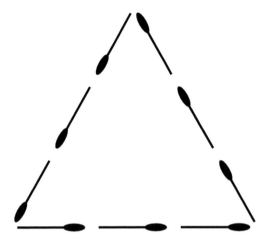

Jigsaw puzzles

Jigsaw puzzles of any kind challenge our spatial perceptions. The following simple puzzles can easily be made by you or by some of your group members. Use a lightweight cardboard to make the puzzles, coloring each one a different color if you want to keep them all together in one bag or box. Each person should have his own puzzle unless you perceive it would be an advantage for two people to work together.

Give each person the four pieces of this puzzle and ask that they make a T from the pieces. This is more difficult than it looks.

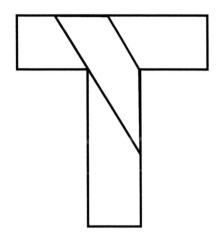

Other jigsaw puzzles to make

◆ Cut up five-inch red hearts into five or six pieces.

◆ Cut up five-inch green shamrocks into five or six pieces.

◆ Use letters from a large poster, cutting them into puzzle pieces.

◆ Make challenging puzzles from magazine pictures that have been pasted on lightweight cardboard.

You will undoubtedly have a number of other ideas. Remember to involve participants in making the puzzles.

If your group finds puzzles interesting and invigorating, there are many commercial jigsaw puzzles available. You might ask the participants to bring one they may have tucked away in a corner of a closet, or suggest that they set the puzzle up at home as a way to sharpen their mental abilities on a daily basis.

Story problems

Your participants will remember the story problem from their grade school days. The following story problems are taken from *New Advanced Arithmetic,* published in 1892. (I found it at a yard sale.)

1. A man has 400 sheep, which he puts in lots of 50 each. How many lots does he make?

2. A stagecoach went 6 miles an hour. How many hours were required to go 30 miles?

3. A school room contains 54 seats arranged in 6 equal rows. How many seats are there in each row?

4. At 3 cents each, how many oranges can be bought for 30 cents?

5. If a school of 42 pupils were divided into 6 equal classes, how many pupils would there be in each class?

6. What is the estimated number of words in a book containing 24 pages, each page averaging 350 words?

7. An 80-acre field was divided into 10-acre lots. How many lots did it make?

8. How many oranges at 3-cents each should be given in exchange for 4 pounds of butter at 15 cents per pound?

9. How many more days are there in the months of March, April, May and June, counted together, than in the months of September and October?

10. If you walked for 2½ hours, how many minutes did you walk?

Most participants will agree that these are fairly easy story problems. Challenge the group members to make up some of their own story problems and then try them out on each other.

Numbers games

Make a set of large number cards (8 inches by 8 inches is a good size) by printing in bold the numbers 1 to 100. There are many games that can be played with these cards.

For example, participants can be seated around a table with paper and pencil. The cards are turned face down on the table, and two players are designated to be card turners. Announce that the goal is to find the sum of the two numbers. One player turns a card face up, and then the second player turns another card up. Each participant writes down the sum of the two numbers. Encourage them to do the math in their head, but accept that many will want to write the numbers down and then add. After 20 such problems, the group members compare answers.

This game may also be played by subtracting or multiplying the two numbers.

Flashcards

Flashcards provide another way to challenge a group in doing numbers. I purchased a set of 90 cards with numbers for division, tried them out with a group and found the group members to be responsive. Most participants prefer to write the answers down rather than respond orally. Actually I think this is better stimulation than if a few people call out the answers while others listen.

Measuring up

Supply participants with pencil and paper and ask them to draw the following without measuring:

1. A line two inches long.
2. A line the length of an average common straight pin.
3. A line the length of a standard pencil.
4. A rectangle the size of a standard playing card.
5. A circle the size of a penny.
6. A circle the size of a 50-cent piece.
7. A line the length of your foot.
8. A line the length of a bobby pin.
9. A rectangle the size of a standard postage stamp.
10. A circle the size of an electrical outlet.

Have several master copies with the measurements drawn out for participants to use to compare with their drawings. Or you may want to have the actual objects available so they can measure them and compare.

Remembering numbers

Put two sets of six numbers on the chalkboard such as:

2   4   8   3   2   5

and

6   3   9   4   5   7

Ask the participants to read these two sets of numbers over at least three times and then try to write them down in the correct order.

If this proves too difficult for your group members, try writing only five numbers in each set. Ask the members to develop their own sets of numbers and keep practicing until their memory gets sharper. Assure them that practice makes a difference and that their inability to memorize is often a result of disuse. (See Words in Place of Numbers in **Chapter 9, "Improving Your Memory,"** for tips on one way of remembering numbers.)

Riddle about numbers

Ask the participants this question:

If one is love and two is sex, what are three and four?

This puzzling question will be amusing and challenging by its simplicity. After a variety of answers have emerged and a number of comments have been made, give the answer (see **Appendix B**).

Appendix A

Pep Talks

The purpose of **Pep Talks** is to give the facilitator short quotes, vignettes and snippets of information you can use to reinforce the importance of keeping the mind active during aging. In our culture most people have a mind-set that aging is all down hill. We have become convinced that our bodies gradually "fall apart" and there is nothing we can do about it. As you might guess, I don't agree with this negative view of aging.

In this section you will find an abundance of positive ideas and attitudes about aging, many of them quotes from books and articles by prominent authors as well as from older people of wisdom. You will also find information about new research on the brain and the benefits of keeping the mind active. Thus this section reinforces the rationale for the importance of doing aerobics of the mind.

This material can be used in a number of ways. The quotes can be woven into aerobics-of-the-mind programs before, during and after a session. Short quotes can be written on the chalkboard. You might want to print some messages on a card and send them home for participants to tape to their bathroom mirrors. I suppose it is the teacher in me looking for one more way to reinforce the message of the chapters—keeping the mind active contributes to physical, emotional and spiritual well-being.

Berman, Phillip L., and **Connie Goldman,** Editors. *The Ageless Spirit.* New York: Ballantine, 1992:

Phyllis Diller:

> Look, I know it isn't always easy to be happy. It's very, very difficult for anyone at any age to keep a positive attitude. But a lot of it is letting go of your fear of change, allowing yourself to try new things. My secret to happiness in old age is to stay busy, to try new things. For example, I've been making great strides in my painting lately. . . . On my seventieth birthday I gave myself a studio; that was my gift to me. (p. 73)

Maggie Kuhn:

> I believe that there has to be a purpose and a goal to life. The secret of thriving and surviving is having a goal. Having a goal is absolutely essential, because it gives you the energy and the drive to do what you must do, and to get up when you feel like staying in bed. I have plenty of goals! On my eightieth birthday, in fact, I vowed to myself that I would do something outrageous at least once a week, and for the past few years I've been able to live up to that promise. (p. 129)

Eda LeShan:

> Did you know that lobsters know when they have to deshell? They get real crowded inside this three-pound shell—they're terribly uncomfortable—and it's not possible for them to go on living if they stay in that shell. So what they do is go out to the sea unprotected, which is very dangerous—they might get hit by a reef, they might be eaten by another lobster or a fish—but they must deshell. That whole, hard shell comes off and the pink membrane that's inside grows and becomes a harder shell, but a bigger one. . . . Going to the reef, even if it's dangerous . . . that really has been my philosophy of life.

. . . You know, if you stay stifled where you are, you're dead before you're dead. So the thing you need more than anything else when you get old is the courage of the lobster. (p. 152)

Norman Vincent Peale:

I think if you continue to work your mind, your mind will work as long as you work it. If you come to age sixty-five and you say, 'Now I'm retired and I'm an old man,' or 'I'm an old woman,' and sit down, your mind will accept your evaluation of yourself and act accordingly. It will get old and tired and sleepy. I still speak, and I speak without notes or without any assistance, and I find that on the platform before an audience, at ninety-three years of age, I can be just as alive as I was at forty. (pp. 215–216)

❖ ❖ ❖

Chopra, Deepak. *Ageless Body, Timeless Mind: The Quantum Alternative to Growing Old.* New York: Harmony, 1998:

By renewing their intention to live active purposeful lives, many elderly people can dramatically improve their motor abilities, strength, agility, and mental responses. (p. 19)

The decline of vigor in old age is largely the result of people expecting to decline; they have unwittingly implanted a self-defeating intention in the form of a strong belief, and the mind-body connection automatically carries out this intention. (p. 19)

Although the image of the body as a mindless machine continues to dominate mainstream Western medicine, there is unquestionable evidence to the contrary. Death rates from cancer and heart disease are probably higher among people in psychological distress, and lower among people who have a strong sense of purpose and well-being. (p. 20)

To despair of growing old makes you grow old faster, while to accept it with grace keeps many miseries, both physical and mental, from your door. The commonsense notion, "You're only as old as you think you are," has deep implications. (p. 21)

As one 80-year-old patient of mine succinctly put it, "People don't grow old. When they stop growing, they become old." New knowledge, new skills, new ways of looking at the world keep mind and body growing, and as long as that happens, the natural tendency to be new at every second is expressed. (p. 24)

In place of the belief that your body decays with time, nurture the belief that your body is new at every moment. In place of the belief that your body is a mindless machine, nurture the belief that your body is infused with the deep intelligence of life, whose sole purpose is to sustain you. These new beliefs are not just nicer to live with; they are true—we experience the joy of life through our bodies, so it is only natural to believe that our bodies are not set against us but want what we want. (p. 26)

George Valliant, a Harvard psychologist, found that "the aging process is learned. People with good mental health teach their bodies to age well; depressed, insecure, and unhappy people teach their bodies to age badly. . . . The greatest threat to life and health is having nothing to live for." (p. 77)

No one knows precisely why some neurons grow 50 dendrites for sending messages while others grow 10,000. One encouraging finding, however, is that by remaining mentally active, older people may actually be growing new dendrites all the time. (p. 245)

Delany, Sarah L., and **A. Elizabeth Delany** with **Amy Hill Hearth.**
Having Our Say. New York: Dell, 1993:

Bessie Delany at 103 said:

> If you asked me the secret to longevity, I would tell you
> that you have to work at taking care of your health. But
> a lot of it's attitude. I'm alive out of sheer determination,
> honey! Sometimes I think it's meanness that keeps me
> going. (p. 17)

Sadie Delany at 101 said:

> Truth is, I've gotten so old I'm starting to get a little bold.
> Not long ago, some young men started hanging out in
> front of our house. They were part of a gang from the
> Bronx. . . . Well, Bessie said to me, "I'll go out there and
> get rid of them," and I said, "No, Bess, for once I'm going
> to handle it." I went out the back door and round to the
> sidewalk where they were hanging out. And I said, "You
> boys better get out of here." . . . And this fella said to me:
> "Just how do you think you're going to make us go?"
> And I said, "My sister is inside and she has her hand on
> the phone to call the police." Of course, this was a little
> white lie because we don't have a phone, but they didn't
> know that. The leader of the group laughed at me and he
> said, "You think the police are gonna come when some
> old nigger woman calls them?" . . . I said, '"Yes, they will
> come, and they will boot you on out of here." Well, they
> grumbled and complained, and finally they left. . . . Bessie
> was kind of surprised that I took those boys on like that.
> To tell the truth, so was I. (pp. 293–294)

Friedan, Betty. A preview of her book *Fountain of Age. Parade Magazine,* June 25, 1992:

> I say let's get on with it—[getting older] is an adventure, not a problem. (p. 14)

Goleman, Daniel. "Studies Suggest Older Minds Are Stronger Than Expected." *New York Times,* February 26, 1966:

> Data from men and women who continue to flourish into their 80s and 90s show that in a healthy brain, any loss of brain cells is relatively modest and largely confined to specific areas, leaving others robust. In fact, about one of every ten people continues to increase in mental abilities like vocabulary through those decades.
>
> "We used to think that you lost brain cells every day of your life everywhere in the brain," said Dr. Marilyn Albert, a psychologist at Massachusetts General Hospital in Boston. "That's just not so—you do have some loss with healthy aging, but not so dramatic, and in very selective brain areas."

Henig, Robin. *The Myth of Senility: The Truth about the Brain and Aging.* Washington, DC: American Association of Retired Persons (AARP), 1991:

> While it is true that the brain changes and slows somewhat as we age, the vast majority of older persons never experience any serious loss of memory or intelligence.

Henig points out that cases of actual "senile dementia" (including Alzheimer's disease) are fairly rare, and that often behaviors mistaken for senility are brought on by other causes, such as improper medication or bodily ailments, and can be successfully treated.

Henig also argues that healthy older persons may adopt "senile" behaviors because they, their families and others expect them to gradually lose mental competence as they grow older—thus perpetuating the myth of senility.

Kalir, Otto. *Grandma Moses.* New York: Abrams, 1973:

Grandma Moses was a pioneer in several ways. She was a pioneer as a farmer's wife in the late 1800s. And she was a pioneer when she became a painter in her 70s. She wasn't the first elderly person to begin exploring her creative potential, but she is an example of one who carried it to its ultimate lengths.

For Grandma Moses, growth meant experiments in new areas and daring to try. Her mind always remained alert, open and eager to take up new suggestions if they appealed to her. When asked why she started to paint in her old age she said, "Well to tell the truth, I had neuritis and arthritis so bad that I could do but little work, but had to keep busy to pass the time away."

Grandma Moses was in a nursing home for awhile just before her 101st birthday. She was mentally alert and full of plans. "As soon as I get back home, I will start painting again." She died in her 101st year, having painted 25 pictures after her hundredth birthday.

Lambert, Pam, Loise Armstrong, and **Joyce Wagner.** "Alzheimer's." *People Magazine,* February 27, 1995:

Are there any effective treatments today for Alzheimer's?

One thing that has been shown to be positive is education. People with higher education levels are less likely to show signs of the disease. . . . [a]s you learn you stimulate the brain, forming more and more connections, thus having more active brain cells in reserve to call on when damage occurs. Many people talk about brain exercises as a way to keep the brain functioning well. Force yourself to use your brain.

Lynch, Dudley. "Brain Aerobics." *American Way,* January 1, 1987:

A crucial aspect of exercising the brain is building bridges to friends, neighbors, relatives, spouses, children, and colleagues. Without company—lots of it—the brain begins to shut down. . . . Cultivate friends now. . .! (p. 34)

Experts suggest exercising the brain by taking it down different routes to work, by walking it along alternate paths to shop, by jogging it down unexplored byways. Otherwise huge swatches of reality may go ignored. (p. 35)

To make sure the brain stays young, one brain trainer urges that you begin immediately to plan a major task or two for each remaining decade of your life. How important is it to achieve all your goals? Not as important as it is to have made them. Much of the new thinking about brain aerobics says that it isn't brains that age; it is attitudes. A busy, changing, well-motivated brain is usually a healthy brain. (p. 35)

Mettler, Molly, and **Donald W. Kemper.** Growing Wiser (a healthwise program developed in Boise, ID), 1986:

Flexibility of the mind is as important as flexibility of the body. Hardening of the arteries is no more damaging than hardening of the attitudes.

Michalko, Michael. *Thinkertoys.* Berkeley, CA: Ten Speed, 1998:

> Give your mind a workout every day. Set yourself an idea
> quota for a challenge you are working on, such as five new
> ideas every day for a week. You'll find the first five are
> the hardest, but these will quickly trigger other ideas.
> ... Having a quota will force you to actively generate
> ideas and alternatives rather than waiting for them to
> occur to you. (p. 12)

Peace Pilgrim. *Peace Pilgrim: Her Life and Work in Her Own Words.*
Santa Fe, NM: Ocean Tree Book, 1991:

> Question: How old are you?

> Along my pilgrimage route many people would ask my
> age. I told them I did not know my age and I did not
> intend to figure it out. I know my birth date. It lingers at
> the fringes of my memory, but I won't divulge it. What
> purpose would it serve? ... I'm very thankful that age
> is out of my mind. As long as I counted birthdays and
> started thinking about getting older, I did get older. Age is
> a state of mind, and I think of myself as ageless. And that's
> my advice to others. Get to be as old as you want to be and
> then stop creating age. (p. 158)

Recer, Paul. "Elderly Couch Potatoes Warned: Use It or Lose It."
The Capitol Times, February 21, 1994

> Just as you can become a physical couch potato, you
> can also become a mental couch potato. It's use it or
> lose it. If you don't engage in intellectual activities you
> can lose the ability, says Dr. K. Warner Schaie. He said
> that he encourages older patients to take on intellectual

challenges and has seen people who were in mental decline actually regain abilities they thought were gone. He said his studies show it is a myth that a decline in mental alertness is inevitable with aging.

Dr. Schaie says that

> Bingo kills the mind. It would be much better to play bridge. It is good for you to do crossword puzzles. The worst thing that could be done is to sit and watch the television.

Sheehy, Gail. *New Passages.* Syndicated column, October 9, 1995:

> Have you asked yourself: What can you make of your next life? . . . What new ventures or adventures can you now dare try? What old shells can you slough off? Are there fatal traps you should avoid? What about those exploratory spiritual journeys you keep putting off? How can you best give back? What investments in learning and change in lifestyle are you willing to undertake to make all these extra years ahead livable? How long do you want to live?

Stern, Caryl. "Who is Old?" *Parade Magazine,* January 21, 1996:

> The bumper crop of centenarians has shattered the assumption that the older you get, the sicker you get. In fact, recent studies show that people in their 90s and older have better overall health than those 10 or 20 years younger.

> "Start rethinking your ideas about who's old. The centenarians are helping to stretch our sense of human

potential," says Dr. Daniel Perry, director of the Alliance for Aging Research in Washington, DC. "If people live to 100, how can you think of a person as used up at 65? We're approaching the day when to be 70 or 80 is going to be middle-aged."

Sylwester, Robert. *A Celebration of Neurons.* Alexandria, VA: Association for Supervision and Curriculum Development, 1995:

Brain imaging technology (such as CAT scans, short for computerized axial tomography) can now clearly identify the brain areas that activate when a subject remembers or responds to something. For example, researchers have monitored the brain activity of subjects who have been asked to respond to nouns with the first verb that comes to mind (e.g., cup might suggest drink). A brain-imaging machine locates and reports the brain areas where the nouns and their related verbs are processed. (p. 12)

Trott, Margot K., with Mark Bricklin. "Better Health with a Twist of the Wrist." *Prevention,* November 1991:

Warning: The Editor-General of Prevention has determined that excessive TV watching can lead to obesity, high cholesterol, disturbed intellectual function and negative emotional states. Keep watching at your own peril.

Turn off your TV and watch your weight and cholesterol plummet, your outlook soar. (p. 41)

Wealti, Alice, senior center participant, Belleville, WI, 1995:

> Yesterday is a memory. Tomorrow is an imagination.
> Today is eternity. Cut two days out of your life, yesterday
> with its mistakes and failures and tomorrow with its fears
> and dreads and live only today. Life is what you make it.
> You can always make it over.

Short quotes from unknown sources

◈ If you think old, you are old.

◈ You don't grow old. You become old by not growing.

◈ Minds are like parachutes, they work best when they
are open.

◈ I admire people who age well more than those who
remain youthful.

◈ Aging is a process of growth, not of decline.

◈ People who have goals live longer than those who don't.

◈ Challenging the brain is vital to the health of the entire body.

◈ Remember that the brain requires workouts just like the rest
of your body.

◈ Try to do something different every day.

◈ Staying active, both mentally and physically—along with eating
a nutritious diet—strengthens the brain, muscles, heart and
immune system.

Appendix B
Answers to Games, Quizzes and Puzzles

Chapter 4 Our Marvelous Brains

Test Your Brain Power

1. **False.** Quite the contrary. There is now evidence that the brain grows stronger, even physically larger, with regular use.

2. **False.** The truth is your memory can actually improve with age.

3. **False.** More often than not these symptoms can be traced to a vitamin, mineral or dietary deficiency. Sometimes medication can create confusion and forgetfulness.

4. **False.** There is a great deal you can do to keep your brain and mind young. Doing aerobics-of-the-mind exercises is one way.

5. **False.** New research is showing that new dendrites can be regenerated.

6. **False.** A number of studies show that creative abilities can be developed as we grow older.

7. **False.** There are a number of methods that can be used to improve your memory.

8. **False.** Females have equal ability to be creative and studies show that they may be *more* creative.

Chapter 14 Fun with Optical illusions

 Most everyone will be able to see the white space as a vase and the black space as forming two faces.

 Some will have difficulty seeing the face of both the young woman and the old woman. Encourage the participants to help each other find the two images.

 Most will answer 16 squares; some will say 17. As you encourage them to think of new ways of forming squares, larger and smaller and in different configurations, most will be able to see up to 30 squares.

 There are 31 total cubes with 13 entirely hidden from view.

 One needs 18 pieces of wood in order to form the cube shown.

 The lines of the triangle are straight.

 The numbers add up to 21 (2, 3, 4, 5 and 7) *or* 75 (7, 23 and 45).

 You should be able to see two people touching their foreheads and a mosque-like structure.

The lower right-hand figure in each group is the same but can be seen as either, depending on the other figures that surround it. These drawings show the importance of context.

 You can see either a seal or a donkey's head. The seal's flippers, which are in the air, also serve as the donkey's ears. The donkey's nostrils are the seal's eyes.

You can see either a duck, coming toward you, or a squirrel seen from the rear. The duck's tail feathers are the squirrel's head, while the duck's head is the squirrel's tail.

 You can see either a rabbit or the back of an American Indian's head. The rabbit's head and ears form the band and single feather at the back of the Indian's head.

Chapter 17 Words, Words, Words

Omitted vowels

1. kitchen
2. garbage
3. basket
4. oatmeal
5. vinegar
6. pepper
7. cinnamon

Scrambled words

Flowers

1. poppy
2. pansy
3. aster

Valentine's Day

1. Cupid
2. Candy
3. Kiss
4. Arrow

Finding letters

There are 36 *f*'s in this paragraph.

Use it or lose it

1. They all use oil.
2. They all have numbers.
3. They all have seats.
4. They all have eyes.
5. They all run.
6. They all get plastered.
7. They are used to carry things.
8. They are on the floor.
9. They are canned.
10. They all have pots.
11. They are stuffed.
12. They all have lenses.
13. They all have skins.
14. They all sparkle.
15. They can be very loud.

Chapter 18 Puzzles and Numbers

Connecting the dots

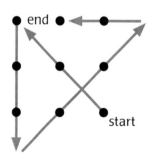

Moving coins

Move coins 1, 7 and 10 to the new positions.

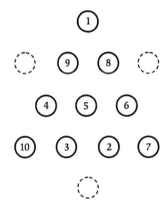

Triangles

The figure has 35 triangles.

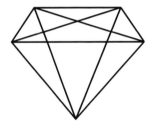

Matchsticks

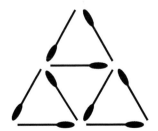

Story problems

1. 8 lots
2. 5 hours
3. 9 seats
4. 10 oranges
5. 7 classes
6. 8,400 words
7. 8 lots
8. 20 oranges
9. 61 days
10. 150 minutes

Riddle about numbers

Three and four are seven.

Appendix c

Resources

Application of knowledge about brain and aging

Cohen, Gene D. *The Creative Age: Awakening Human Potential in the Second Half of Life.* New York: Avon, 2000.

This world-renowned psychiatrist and researcher speaks to us of the creative power generated by age and experience, and shows us how to tap this inner source to enrich, even transform, our lives through middle age and beyond. For him, age can become an asset if we can awaken the creativity that gives us fresh hope and renewed vigor. Contains many ideas for developing creative abilities.

Eiffert, Stephen D. *Cross-train Your Brain: A Mental Fitness Program for Maximizing Creativity and Achieving Success.* New York: American Management Association, 1999.

This book comes out of the business world, but there are many ideas relevant to optimum aging. For example, "If you love books, set aside time to learn to work with your hands. If you are a musician, play a word game such as Scrabble." In short, train your brain by participating in activities that expand its powers. You can expand your brain power in millions of little ways.

Engleman, Marge. Aerobics of the Mind Card Pack. Verona, WI: Attainment, 2001.

A set of 100 laminated 4″ x 6″ cards contains challenging exercises for a healthy brain. The cards can be used by individuals or small groups to help keep the mind active. Categories include Wake Up Your Brain, Words, Memory, Numbers, Creative Problem Solving, Art and Imagination, Puzzles, Seeing, Smelling and Hearing, and Double Mind.

Gelb, Michael J. *How to Think Like Leonardo da Vinci.* New York: Dell, 1998.

This is billed as a brilliant, practical guide to awakening and training our vast, unused resources of intelligence and ability. With da Vinci as your inspiration, you will discover new ways of thinking and behaving. Exercises deal with problem solving, creative thinking, self-expression, enjoying the world around you and harmonizing body and mind.

Goldman, Robert, and **Ronald Klatz.** *Brain Fitness.* New York: Broadway Books, 1999.

Goldman is director of the American Academy of Anti-Aging Medicine and has at his fingertips the latest scientific research on what each of us can do, not only to retain all our mental powers as long as we live, but also to actually strengthen and improve our mind power as we age. Chapters include Fight Alzheimer's Disease, Supercharge Your Memory, Sharpen Your Intelligence, De-Stress Your Mind, and Control Mood Swings.

Katz, Lawrence C. *Keep Your Brain Alive: Eighty-three Neurobic Exercises.* New York: Workman, 1999.

The book claims to be a unique brain exercise program based on the latest neuroscience research. These deceptively simple exercises help stimulate the production of nutrients that grow brain cells to keep the brain younger and stronger. Neurobics uses the five senses in unexpected ways and shakes up everyday routines.

Noir, Michel, and Bernard Croisile. *Dental Floss for the Mind: A Complete Program for Boosting Your Brain Power.* New York: McGraw-Hill, 2005.

Written by a noted cognitive scientist and a top neurologist, this book features more than 100 creative and fun exercises that target the five key cognitive areas of memory, attention, language skills, spatial recognition and reasoning ability.

Short, Cynthia S. *Grow Dendrites Forever: The Brain Fitness Kit.* Author, 1998.

This workbook combines brain fitness exercises for strengthening your sensory and memory skills with a blueprint for creating new dendrite growth. The author offers a wealth of practical tips, techniques and exercises for keeping your brain alive and growing throughout life. It is stimulating, clearly written and fun to use.

Snowdon, Parlette. *The Brain Workout Book.* New York: Evans, 1997.

"Use it or lose it" is as true of our mental faculties as it is of our physical abilities. But often our brain stimulation is not very balanced. This book provides exercises for all the major brain functions at different levels. The exercises are usable and fun.

Wetzel, Kathryn, and **Kathleen Harmeyer.** *Mind Games: The Aging Brain and How to Keep It Healthy.* Stamford, CT: Thomson Learning, 2000.

This book includes proven techniques that will help rejuvenate your mind. It is based on solid university research that produced "stunning results." Looks at how individuals prefer to learn and contains a section on how the brain functions.

Winter, Arthur, and **Ruth Winter.** *Brain Workout: Easy Ways to Power Up Your Memory, Sensory Perception, and Intelligence.* New York: St. Martin's Griffin, 1997.

Until recently, it was believed that as the years pass, the brain inevitably deteriorates in all its functions. According to Dr. Arthur Winter, neurosurgeon and director of the New Jersey Neurological Institute, studies show that the brain can continue to develop and repair itself, even in old age, and that with simple daily exercises, the proper diet and the right kind of mental stimulation, you can strengthen and maintain your brain's power to near maximum capacity.

Background reading about brain and aging

Birren, James E., and **K. Warner Schaie** (Editors). *Handbook of the Psychology of Aging* (4th ed.). San Diego: Academic Press, 2001.

A heavy-duty academic volume that is the definitive reference source for information on the psychology of adult development and aging.

Carper, Jean. *Your Miracle Brain.* New York: Quill Books, 2000.

The author, a leading authority on health and nutrition, tells you how to mold your brain to optimize memory, intelligence, mental achievement and mood by eating the right foods and taking specific brain-boosting supplements. She is acclaimed as one of the most reliable authorities on ways of improving health by natural means.

Chopra, Deepak. *Ageless Body, Timeless Mind: The Quantum Alternative to Growing Old.* New York: Harmony, 1998.

If you have time to read only one book that relates a positive attitude about aging, read this one.

Conari Press [Editors]. *Random Acts of Kindness.* Berkeley, CA: Conari, 2002.

A little book that inspires people of all ages to reach out as a way to enhance life.

Friedan, Betty. *The Fountain of Age.* New York: Simon and Schuster, 1993.

This book breaks through the mystique of age-as-problem and points out how one can grow old and evolve into a new and exciting dimension of personhood.

The Hen Co-op. *Growing Old Disgracefully.* Freedom, CA: Crossing, 1994.

Written by six women between the ages of 60 and 75, this book challenges stereotypes and suggests ways to make life at any age more joyous and creative. A delightful book!

Lee, James L., and **Charles J. Pulvino.** *Educating the Forgotten Half.* Dubuque, IA: Kendall/Hunt, 1978.

Focuses on structured activities for learning, emphasizing the use of the right brain.

Lewthwaite, Nancy J. *Mental Aerobics* (rev. ed.). Victoria, BC: Author, 1992.

Available from Mental Aerobics, 4417 Torrington Road, Victoria, BC, Canada, V8N 4N8. About $50. A spiral-bound resource manual of mentally stimulating group activities for seniors. Includes quizzes, theme week and special event activities.

Lewthwaite, Nancy J. *More Mental Aerobics.* Victoria, BC: Author, 1999.

Mahoney, David, and **Richard Restak.** *The Longevity Strategy: How to Live to 100 Using the Brain-Body Connection.* New York: Wiley, 1998.

The brain-body connection is the interaction among three factors: The health of our brains, our attitudes and thought patterns, and our physical health. The authors explain the vital importance of handling stress properly, lifelong education and mental activity, the social connection, physical exercise and rearranging your brain's hardwiring toward optimism. The book contains 31 practical things to do that will enhance your longevity.

Michalko, Michael. *Thinkertoys* (2nd ed.). Berkeley, CA: Ten Speed, 1998.

Idea-generating tools, tested and proven at some of America's top businesses.

Perls, Thomas, and **Margery Hutter Silver.** *Living to 100: Lessons in Living to Your Maximum Potential at Any Age.* New York: Basic Books, 1999.

These two Harvard Medical School researchers have studied more than one hundred centenarians, interviewing them in their homes, scrutinizing their family trees and assessing their physical and mental health. By identifying lifestyle patterns they indicate that learning new skills can actually renew or extend the life of brain cells.

Ratey, John. *A User's Guide to the Brain.* New York: Vintage Books, 2001.

The author, a clinical professor of psychiatry at Harvard Medical School, explains the human brain's workings and paves the way for a better understanding of how the brain affects who we are. He provides insight into the basic structure and chemistry of the brain and demonstrates how its systems shape our perceptions, emotions and behavior.

Restak, Richard. *Mozart's Brain and the Fighter Pilot: Unleashing Your Brain's Potential.* New York: Three Rivers, 2001.

Unlike other organs that eventually wear out with repeated and sustained use, the brain actually improves the more we challenge it. Packed with practical advice drawn from history, literature and science, this book provides 28 informative and realistic steps we can all take to improve our brainpower.

Restak, Richard. *The Secret Life of the Brain.* Washington, DC: Joseph Henry, 2001.

The book is a companion to the television series brought to PBS (Public Broadcasting System) by the award-winning producer David Grubin. It is a comprehensive exploration of recent discoveries and their impact on human development. Beautiful photographs and original illustrations combine with a vivid and compelling narrative to bring this fascinating science of the brain to life.

Robbins, Jim. *A Symphony in the Brain.* New York: Atlantic Monthly Press, 2000.

Using electroencephalograms (EEGs) and computerized biofeedback equipment, neurofeedback clinicians train patients to function in brain frequencies they don't normally use. This exercise strengthens the brain and the rest of the nervous system, which in turn has powerful effects on the entire body. Although the medical profession remains skeptical, the procedure appears to be on the verge of bursting onto the nation's radar screen.

Rowe, John W., and **Robert L. Kahn.** *Successful Aging: Older People Can Increase Their Mental Abilities.* New York: Pantheon Books, 1998.

This is a MacArthur Foundation Study, begun in 1987, which explains that successful aging is determined not by genetic inheritance—as common wisdom has it—but by individual lifestyle choices in diet, exercise, the pursuit of mental challenges, self-efficacy and involvement with other people.

Sher, Barbara. *It's Only Too Late If You Don't Start Now: How to Create Your Second Life at Any Age.* New York: Dell, 1999.

This best-selling author combines step-by-step exercises with motivational techniques, reminding you of the dreams you abandoned along the path to adulthood. There are dozens of ways to recapture your freedom, reclaim a sense of wonder and embark on an amazing new beginning.

Snowden, David. *Aging with Grace: What the Nun Study Teaches Us About Leading Longer, Healthier, and More Meaningful Lives.* New York: Bantam, 2001.

These nuns, from the nationwide Order of the School Sisters of Notre Dame, live to an average age of 85. Brain exercise is a way of life at the nunneries. The women live by the principle that an idle mind is the devil's plaything. A total of 678 nuns have willed their brains for research striving to understand and develop treatment for Alzheimer's.

Sylwester, Robert. *A Celebration of Neurons.* Alexandria, VA: Association for Supervision and Curriculum Development, 1995.

Helps to understand the brain's basic working and how to use that understanding to work with people.

von Oech, Roger. *A Whack on the Side of the Head.* New York: Warner, 1998.

Focuses on mental blocks to innovation and shows what can be done about them.

Zdenek, Marilee. *The Right-brain Experience: An Intimate Program to Free the Powers of Your Imagination.* New York: McGraw-Hill, 1996.

Ways to stimulate creativity, maximize productivity and revolutionize the approach to problem solving.

Games

Boyd, Neva L. *Handbook of Recreational Games.* New York: Dover, 1973.

Contains many of the games we have played for years, plus new ones.

Cox, Claire. *Rainy Day Fun for Kids.* New York: Association Press, 1962.

A classic, containing a wide variety of games appropriate for all ages.

Russell, Ken, and **Philip Carter.** *Number Puzzles.* New York: Foulsham, 1993.

Graded at three different levels to build skills.

Most large book stores have a Games section. If you haven't looked lately, you'll be surprised at the abundance of game books.

Memory

Fogler, Janet, and **Lynn Stern.** *Improving Your Memory* (rev. ed.). Baltimore, MD: The Johns Hopkins University Press, 1994.

Fun and easy to read. Includes practical information and proven methods to improve memory. *Modern Maturity* says, "The finest handbook we've seen on the subject."

Green, Cynthia R. *Total Memory Workout: Eight Easy Steps to Maximum Memory Fitness.* New York: Bantam Books, 1999.

Of the many recently published books related to memory, this one is a star. Dr. Green outlines her simple and effective program to achieve maximum memory fitness in just eight easy lessons. Each lesson focuses on one aspect of memory followed by a series of specific "memorizes" designed to build memory muscle.

Higbee, Kenneth L. *Your Memory: How It Works and How to Improve It.* New York: Marlowe, 2001.

Here you will find real-world, practical advice on how to improve your memory. Dr. Higbee reveals how to incorporate many simple memory techniques in your everyday life and claims you will benefit immediately from your greatly improved memory. The material is backed by extensive research and is well documented.

Schafer, Edith Nalle. *Our Remarkable Memory.* Washington, DC: Starrhill, 1992.

A fine little book on memory—understanding how it works, losing it, improving it.

Small, Gary. *The Memory Bible: An Innovative Strategy for Keeping Your Brain Young.* New York: Hyperion, 2002.

This much-quoted author includes in this book a "brain diet" of memory-protective foods, a guide to the most effective drugs and treatments available, a workbook section and a chapter on getting fit with mental aerobics.

Winter, Arthur, and **Ruth Winter.** *Brain Workout: Easy Ways to Power Up Your Memory, Sensory Perception, and Intelligence.* New York: St. Martin Griffin, 1997.

Contains many helpful exercises to be used on a daily basis to give the mind stimulation and to strengthen and maintain your brain's power to near maximum capacity throughout your life.

Organizations and publications

Activities, Adaptation, and Aging. The Haworth Press, 10 Alice Street, Binghamton, New York, NY 13904, www.haworthpressinc.com

A journal (that sometimes publishes books) which provides information and activities for those working with older adults and people with disabilities.

Activity Director's Guide. Eymann Publications, Box 612, Cedar Falls, IA 50613, www.care4elders.com.

Newsletters containing ideas for activity programs.

American Society on Aging, 833 Market Street, Suite 512, San Francisco, CA 54103-1824.

Publishes a quarterly newsletter of this organization's Older Adult Education Network. Up-to-date information on aging.

Bi-Focal Productions, 809 Williamson Street, Madison, WI 53703, phone: 800-568-5357.

Provides a variety of kits, which include slides, games, songs, recipes, skits, etc.—all designed to bring back memories of the past.

Creative Education Foundation, 289 Bay Road, Hadley, MA 01035, phone: 800-447-2774.

Publishes a valuable quarterly, *The Journal of Creative Behavior,* and stocks many basic books on creativity and creative problem solving. Ask for their free catalog. A marvelous resource!

Dover Publications, 31 East 2nd Street, Mineola, NY 11501.

Publishers of books on art activities, mathematics, puzzles, brain teasers, etc. Order their free catalog at www.store.yahoo. com/doverpublications/.

McGoff Enterprises, 3824 North Airport Drive, Stillwater, OK 74075, phone: 405-372-0810, website: www.mcgoff@cowboy.net.

They produce board games designed for seniors.

Museum One, 35 Dover Chester Road, Randolph, NJ 07869, phone: 800-524-1730.

Provides outreach visual art programs and educational materials to providers of services to senior citizens.

The National Association of Activity Professionals, PO Box 5530. Seviervielle, TX 37864.

Active, associate and subscriber memberships are available in this association that represents, exclusively, activity professionals in geriatric settings. Annual membership includes a monthly newsletter. Write or email for more information at info@thenaap.com.

National Gallery of Art, Publications Mail Order Department, 2000 B South Club Drive, Landover, MD 20785, phone: 301-322-5900.

Prints of works of art in their collection. Call for color reproductions catalog. Also offers its collection of films, slide programs and video cassettes free of charge for five working days to educational institutions, community groups and individuals throughout the U.S. A free catalog is available by contacting Extension Programs, National Gallery of Art, Washington, DC 20565, phone: 202-737-4215, email: der-info@nga.gov.

Senior Net, 121 Second St. 7th Floor, San Francisco, CA 94105, phone: 415-495-4990, website: www.seniornet.org.

Senior Net is a nonprofit national organization whose goal is to create a community of computer-using older adults. Individuals who are age 55 and older are eligible to be members. Offers computer instruction and access to an on-line telecommunications network.

Other useful books related to words

Felleman, Hazel, Compiler. *Best Loved Poems of the American People.* New York: Doubleday, 1936, 1989.

If you want to use a poem in your sessions, here are all the golden oldies.

Slung, Michele. *Momilies.* New York: Ballantine, 1985.

Things one's mother used to say can inspire participants to remember their favorite "momilies" and to create some new ones of their own.

Zimmerman, William. *A Book of Questions.* Madison, WI: Bi-Focal Productions, 1984.

Designed for older adults, this book of questions will provide discussion topics for months.

Visuals and art

Block, J. Richard, and **Harold Yuker.** *Can You Believe Your Eyes?* New York: Gardner, 1989.

Over 250 illusions and other visual oddities. Great stimulation and fun!

Edwards, Betty. *Drawing on the Right Side of the Brain.* Los Angeles: Tarcher, 1979.

An art educator discovers a new way to unlock creative potential in the visual arts.

Gawain, Shakti. *Creative Visualization.* New York: Bantam, 1982.

An introduction and workbook for the art of using mental energy to transform and improve health, beauty, prosperity, relationships and the fulfillment of desires.

The Jumbo Book of Hidden Pictures. Honesdale, PA: Bell Books, 1992.

Hidden pictures provide hours of fascinating and challenging fun. Stimulates spatial abilities.

Kuemmerlein, Kenneth. *Exploring Ideas in Art.* Madison, WI: University of Wisconsin Board of Regents, 1981.

A book for leaders that shows how to approach art with any group and make it interesting.

O'Neill, Mary. *Hailstones and Halibut Bones.* New York: Doubleday, 1961.

An exploration of the spectrum of colors in poetry. A gem!

Rottger, Ernst. *Creative Paper Design.* New York: Reinhold, 1961.

You will find numerous examples of how paper, inexpensive and easy to work with, can be cut, pieced, pasted, folded and interwoven into enchanting forms and useful objects.

Striker, Susan, and **Edward Kimmel.** *The Anti-Coloring Book.* New York: Henry Holt, 1984.

A series of paperbacks that includes many projects that stimulate the imagination and spark creativity.

Websites

Websites come and go. I have my favorites, listed here, but to find some of your own, use your favorite search engine and enter words like "brainteaser," "puzzle," "logical challenges," "illusions" and so on.

www.agenet.com   Background reading and many mentally stimulating exercises.

www.brainbashers.com   Unique collection of puzzles, games and optical illusions that is updated regularly.

www.dana.org   Brain resources for seniors: health, education and aging.

www.dse.nl/puzzle/index_us   Puzzles marked with stars denoting degree of difficulty.

www.neurobics.com   Neurobic exercises to help prevent memory loss and increase mental fitness.

www.rhymezone.com   Enter a word and retrieve all the words that rhyme with it. You can also ask for antonyms, synonyms and similar sounding words, among other features.

Words

Brandreth, Gyles. *The Biggest Tongue Twister Book in the World.* New York: Sterling, 1978.

You'll be amazed and amused.

Gleason, Norma. *Fun with Word Puzzles.* New York: Dover, 1992.

A treasure of 132 entertaining word games and puzzles, including cryptograms, scrambled-word puzzles, little acrostics, word searches, word squares, letter mazes, little crosswords, and much more.

Good 'N' Easy Crosswords. Fort Washington, PA: Harle.

These crosswords are easy to solve and quick to do. They would provide a good beginning for those who have not done crosswords before. Available at newsstands or as a subscription; 12 issues a year.

Keller, Charles. *Tongue Twisters.* New York: Simon and Schuster, 1989.

Russell, Ken, and **Philip Carter.** *The Complete Guide to Word Games and Word Play.* New York: Foulsham, 1995.

A rich resource for word games and other activities with words.

Seek-a-word. Fort Washington, PA: Stavrolex.

These are large print puzzles, easy to read. Available at newsstands or as a subscription; 12 issues a year.

This 'N' That, See-a-word. Racine, WI: Merrigold.

> To play see-a-word you look up and down, across and back, diagonally in both directions. These word puzzles are good mind stimulators, easier than crosswords.

There are endless publications of crossword puzzles, including daily newspapers. They are a good way to do mental exercise on a regular basis.

Notes

Chapter 1 Creating the Climate

1. These rules were used at the White House Conference on Aging, May 1995.

Chapter 2 Warm-Ups

1. Weil, Andrew, MD. *Spontaneous Healing.* New York: Knopf, 1995.

2. Lee, James, and Charles Pulvino. *Educating the Forgotten Half.* Dubuque, IA: Kendall/Hunt, 1978.

Chapter 3 What Is Aerobics of the Mind?

1. Adapted from the *Journal of Creative Behavior* 14(2): Second Quarter, 1980.

Chapter 4 Our Marvelous Brains

1. Schafer, Edith Nalle. *Our Remarkable Memory.* Washington, DC: Starrhill, 1992.

2. Michaud, Ellen, Russell Wild and the Editors of *Prevention. Boost Your Brain Power.* Emmaus, PA: Rodale, 1991.

3. Adapted from exercises in Zdenek, Marilee. *The Right-brain Experience: An Intimate Program to Free the Powers of Your Imagination.* New York: McGraw-Hill, 1983.

Chapter 6 Color, Wonderful Color

1. From *Hailstones and Halibut Bones* by O'Neill, Mary, and Leonard Weisgard, III. ©1961 by Mary LeDuc O'Neill. Used by permission of Doubleday, a division of Bantam Doubleday Dell Publishing Group, Inc.

Chapter 7 Trees

1. *The World Book Encyclopedia.* Chicago, IL: World Book, 1990.

Chapter 8 Will You Be My Valentine?

1. *The World Book Encyclopedia.* Chicago, IL: World Book, 1990.

Chapter 9 Improving Your Memory

1. Fogler, Janet, and Lynn Stern. *Improving Your Memory* (rev. ed.). Baltimore, MD: The Johns Hopkins University Press, 1994.

2. Adapted from the *Journal of Creative Behavior* 14(2): Second Quarter, 1980.

Chapter 11 Stimulating Discussions

1. Adapted from The Hen Co-op. *Growing Old Disgracefully.* Freedom, CA: Crossing, 1994.

2. Some questions adapted from Zimmerman, William. *A Book of Questions.* Madison, WI: Bi-Focal Productions, 1984.

Chapter 12 Right Brain Exercises

1. Adapted from Lee, James, and Charles Pulvino. *Educating the Forgotten Half.* Dubuque, IA: Kendall/Hunt, 1978.

2. Adapted from Kuemmerlein, Kenneth. *Exploring Ideas in Art.* Madison, WI : University of Wisconsin Board of Regents, 1981.

3. Adapted from Rottger, Ernst. *Creative Paper Design.* New York: Reinhold, 1961.

Chapter 14 Fun with Optical Illusions

1. Adapted from Block, J. Richard, and Harold Yuker. *Can You Believe Your Eyes?* New York: Gardner, 1989.

2. From Hanson (1958), found in Block and Yuker, 1989.

3. From Eisher (1968a), found in Block and Yuker, 1989.

Chapter 15 Sharpening the Senses

1. Michaud, Ellen, Russell Wild, and the Editors of *Prevention. Boost Your Brain Power.* Emmaus, PA: Rodale, 1991.

2. "Sniffing Out the Sense of Smell." *National Geographic,* March 1996.

Chapter 17 Words, Words, Words

1. Swerdlow, Joel L. "Quiet Miracles of the Brain." *National Geographic,* June 1995.

Mental Workout Card Set

This two-box set of Attainment's mental workout cards provides hours of creative activities for older adults. Ideal for one-on-one or small groups. These cards reflect many of the exercises discussed in *Aerobics of the Mind*.

Thinking Cards are specially designed for older adults with Mild Cognitive Impairment and early Alzheimer's Disease. These 100 exercises, activities and memory tips keep the mind active and strengthen existing skills while users have fun! A colorful photo on the back of each card illustrates its topic and encourages discussion. Larger type and simple text encourages participation. Developed by Marge Engelman, Ph.D., Danielle Leuthje, MSSW, Gail Petersen, Ph.D., and Kim Petersen, M.D.

Mental Fitness Cards include 100 challenging activities that encourage users to do aerobics of the mind. Developed by Dr. Marge Engelman, these cards cover 12 categories like Wake up Your Brain, Memory, Numbers, Words, Creative Problem Solving, Puzzles, Brainstorming and more. Each card makes suggestions, presents activities or outlines strategies for keeping the mind stimulated.

Available from Attainment Co. Inc.
1-800-327-4269
www.AttainmentCompany.com